T0364413

THE
SALTWATER
EDGE

THE
SALTWATER
EDGE

TIPS AND TACTICS FOR SALTWATER FLY FISHING

NICK CURCIONE

STACKPOLE
BOOKS

Guilford, Connecticut

Published by Stackpole Books
An imprint of Globe Pequot
Trade Division of The Rowman & Littlefield Publishing Group, Inc.
4501 Forbes Boulevard, Suite 200, Lanham, Maryland 20706
www.rowman.com

Distributed by
NATIONAL BOOK NETWORK
800-462-6420

Copyright © 2017 Nick Curcione
Photos by Nick Curcione unless otherwise noted

All rights reserved. No part of this book may be reproduced in any form or by any electronic or mechanical means, including information storage and retrieval systems, without written permission from the publisher, except by a reviewer who may quote passages in a review.

British Library Cataloguing in Publication Information Available

Library of Congress Cataloging-in-Publication Data Available

ISBN 978-0-8117-1909-4 (paperback)
ISBN 978-0-8117-6593-0 (e-book)

The paper used in this publication meets the minimum requirements of American National Standard for Information Sciences—Permanence of Paper for Printed Library Materials, ANSI/NISO Z39.48-1992.

Printed in the United States of America

CONTENTS

ACKNOWLEDGMENTS

I find a bit of irony in the fact that compared to a book's chapters, the acknowledgement section seldom encompasses more than a page or two. In this sense I don't think it's too farfetched to compare it to a snapshot of an angler cradling a prize catch. Despite the visual impact of the photo, it only portrays the endpoint of a successful encounter. Nothing is captured detailing all the preparatory steps, the time, the effort, and the practice that culminated in the catch.

This is not to be construed as an apology, because where books are concerned, most readers simply wouldn't be interested in this kind of input. Similarly, with the possible exception of serious anglers, most folks viewing the photo wouldn't question the process by which the feat was accomplished. But when you are trying to convey information in book form, even with a single author the presumption is that the work is not the product of a completely solitary effort, and a notion of fairness that evolved into protocol dictates that mention be made of those individuals who were an important influence on the writer's work. The shortcoming is that the reader often fails to get a sense of the full measure of the impact these others had on the author.

With that said and at the risk of omission, I want to assure you the reader that all the individuals I'm about to mention had a significant impact on my fishing career. They are (or were in the case of two who passed away) close friends, and I treasure the time I spend with them on and off the water. To avoid the impression of an implied ranking, they are listed alphabetically. Here I want to give special thanks to Travis Vander Linden, my stepson and a talented graphic artist who rendered all the knot illustrations.

The late Bill Barnes, who taught me a great deal about fishing the salt with fly gear.

Captain Joe Blados, a standup guy who knows the east end of Long Island like the proverbial back of his hand.

Dan Blanton, West Coast fly-fishing guru and a longtime multitalented buddy with the best fly-fishing website in the country.

Ed Jaworowski, a wizard with the fly rod and a man with unbounded enthusiasm and mastery in everything he sets his mind to.

The late Harry Kime, who opened my eyes to the fishery in Baja.

Lefty Kreh, who aside from his encyclopedic knowledge of the sport, taught me a lot about life. I regard him as a second father, and I think that says it all.

Captain Scott Leon, my former editor who did a lot for my writing career and is someone who is always there when I need him.

John Loo, we go back to when Southern California saltwater fly fishing was in its infancy, and you've never lost your enthusiasm.

Doug Lum, a humble virtuoso of Oahu's shallow-water flats who has unselfishly guided me to many of his favorite spots.

Bob Popovics, a master at the vise, a superb caster, an aficionado of the surf, a great restaurateur, and, most important of all, a man who is like a brother to me.

Andy and Lily Renzetti, purveyors of exquisite fly-tying vises and accessories who genuinely care about the sport.

My buddies at San Francisco's Golden Gate Casting Ponds who introduced me to Spey and Skagit casting: Burt Rances, Frank Chen, Al Tom, and Sigi Mo.

The folks at Temple Fork Outfitters (TFO), the best company I've ever been associated with.

Captain Jim White, I can never forget the schools of stripers and blues you've guided me to in Rhode Island.

Captain Roan Zumfelde, thanks for the great times and all you've taught me about the fishery in southwest Florida.

Last, but not least, my lovely wife, Kathy, who keeps me healthy, is a constant source of inspiration, and serves as my live GPS.

PREFACE

Over 20 years have elapsed since Lefty Kreh's classic publication on saltwater fly fishing. Since then there have been numerous offerings on the subject, but even the ones that purport to offer a comprehensive overview often lack detailed descriptions of one or another critical aspects of the sport and I include in that list two of my own previous publications, *The Orvis Guide to Saltwater Fly Fishing* (1994) and *Tug-O-War: A Fly Fisher's Game* (2001).

We use it often in reference to fly fishing, but there has never been a consideration of exactly what that entails when we venture out on the water with fly gear. A related concern that is seldom mentioned is the mindset with which we approach this undertaking despite the fact that one's attitude can have a critical impact on the enjoyment we derive from this pastime.

On the instructional level, though growing in popularity, to date there hasn't been a great deal of material devoted to the use of two-handed rods in saltwater fly fishing. A stripping basket may seem like a mundane accessory, and most works only make slight reference to it. The same may be said for something like polarized glasses. How do they function, and what are the best choices for different fishing situations? Knots—which ones are most useful in salt water, and what is the simplest way of tying them? Shooting heads—why use them, and how do you cast them?

The motivation for the present work is to fill in some of these gaps based on over four decades of experience fishing the salt with fly gear. Instead of writing an all-inclusive, albeit general work on the sport, my objective is to offer a detailed account of time-tested methods, strategies, and techniques, many of which I have learned and some that I've developed, that will enable you to successfully fly fish in any marine environment. This book is unique in terms of both the nature and the depth of the subjects it discusses. Based on my academic background as a sociologist, as mentioned above, I've included two "outside the box" issues that deal with dimensions of the fly-fishing enterprise seldom if ever mentioned in the fly-fishing literature. Chapter 1 deals with both concerns. It begins with a consideration of the fundamental elements of what it means to engage in the pastime of fly fishing. This transitions into a short excursion as to the very meaning of what constitutes a sporting activity and how it applies to those who seek to identify themselves as fly fishers. In a similar sociological vein, the chapter takes up another subject rarely discussed in the fishing literature, that being the role that one's attitude and personal perspective play in fly-fishing experiences.

As a sample of the material covered in the succeeding chapters, you will find detailed accounts of vital preparation steps, including what to look for and how to look. In addition to guiding you through proper fly line selection, the chapter on lines takes an in-depth look at shooting heads and the steps involved in casting sinking lines. The recent development of using two-handed rods in saltwater is taken up in chapter 5, along with a discussion of different two-handed casting techniques and fishing applications. A chapter is devoted to the important issue of line management, along with detailed instructions for building a stripping basket. The chapter on knots is a primer on the connections you need to know, with a section on how to construct a very simple, useful knot-tying tool. The chapter on flies not only is intended to help simplify the fly selection process, but also discusses a readily available, economical tying material, along with instructions for constructing a revolutionary popper system.

My years of teaching experience taught me that one of the most interesting and effective ways to convey information is by way of example, and throughout the book I use antidotes from my fishing experiences to illustrate various fly-fishing techniques and strategies. The ultimate goal is to enrich your experience when you venture into a saltwater fly zone.

1

Fly Fishing as Sport

CAPTAIN JOE BLADOS

Any member of the tuna family makes for an exciting challenge on fly tackle. A very popular member of that clan is this false albacore taken on the east end of Long Island's north shore.

Some years back the editor of a now-defunct fly-fishing magazine wrote an article on fly-fishing rules that brought to mind some issues I dealt with in my former career as a professor of sociology. One of the specialized areas in this discipline is the sociology of sport, and over the years I wrote a number of papers that examined various facets of what my colleagues liked to refer to as recreational fishing. I regret that I never had the opportunity to tell that editor personally, but the one definition that best captures the very essence of what it means to engage in a

1

sporting activity did not hail from the scholarly literature. Instead, it came from the late outdoor writer Charlie Waterman.

Charlie defined sport as an activity that is governed by a set of self-imposed limitations. Basically what this involves is an attempt to increase the level of difficulty in whatever one is trying to accomplish. It is the dual process of confronting and, if successful, overcoming the challenge that gives us a measure of satisfaction. In this sense, in terms of desired outcomes, a sporting activity is not highly rational because we do not seek the most efficient means to accomplish the goal.

Sport fishing is a classic example. The one dimension that differentiates the commercial from the recreational angler is that the former seeks the most efficient means to capture fish. Commercial fishermen can and do derive a great deal of satisfaction from their work. But the bottom line is that they are not in it for fun or recreation. To survive economically they must catch fish, and they try to do it in the most efficient way possible. The rules and regulations they are bound by are mainly imposed by outside agencies like state and federal governments. Within the framework of these regulations, commercial fishermen concentrate on trying to maximize the efficiency of their fish-catching efforts. In this sense the commercial fisherman is said to be primarily goal oriented whereas the recreational angler, ideally, is means oriented. In fishing for sport, catching fish is not regarded as the sole purpose of the activity. Instead, a great deal of importance is also placed on the method used to catch the fish.

In the tuna fishery, for example, the old jack pole method, which simply consisted of a Calcutta pole, a length of line, and a feathered jig (think of it as an extreme form of tenkara fishing), has been supplanted by the much more efficient purse seine net to capture a school. When I first moved to Southern California, I had the opportunity to fish albacore on a jack pole boat, and the sensation of pulling on fish like these with a pole and line is an incredibly exciting experience. But it's seldom practiced anymore because it cannot compete with the productivity afforded by purse seines.

As sport anglers we are also bound by state and federal regulations. But in addition to these formal laws that govern issues like quota, size, seasonal, and species restrictions, we subject ourselves to an additional set of self-imposed regulations, like the ones laid down by the International Game Fish Association (IGFA). Unlike the formal regulations imposed by government agencies, we are free to choose to follow or completely ignore these rules. So why would anyone elect to fish by these rules? Basically for the same reason one would choose to climb to a mountaintop instead of ascending it by helicopter: The challenge and difficulty in making the climb is the attraction that draws some to attempt it.

For those who want to fish primarily for the pure fun of it, the IGFA has established rules regarding rod, reel, line, and leader specifications as well as presentation and fish-fighting methods, all of which are intended to add to the element of challenge. If you choose to fly fish by these rules, you are choosing to handicap yourself even more so than sport anglers using conventional and spinning tackle. For example, you cannot use bait. You cannot even sweeten the offering with something like fish scent. Regardless of how convincing your flies may look or perform, as an old television commercial used to say, "It's not nice to fool Mother Nature." In terms of catching fish, the hard fact is that in the vast majority of cases, bait, either dead or alive, is far more effective than any unnatural substitute.

Do you want to significantly increase your chances of taking a permit on a fly rod? Put on a live crab instead of that beautifully crafted imitation and your chances will improve dramatically. Can't get a roosterfish to eat your streamer? Do what a friend of mine did in Baja some years ago and impale a live sardine on it and watch what happens. The irony of this latter incident is that the guy is an accomplished big-game bow hunter who would only resort to a rifle if his life were in imminent danger. In this case he wasn't proud of what he did and sheepishly admitted that he wanted to experience the sensation of fighting this fish on fly gear. His casting needed a lot of work, and he felt live bait was his only option. In that sense he accomplished what he set out to do. Aside from using a live sardine, he can claim that he caught roosterfish on fly gear. However, by IGFA standards at least, this feat is not recognized as fly fishing.

A second major consideration raised in that magazine article and related to the roosterfish incident is the IGFA requirement to present a totally artificial offering by casting it, not trolling it or simply dropping it in the water once a fish has been enticed alongside the boat. Here again we have a level-of-difficulty issue. Most people who take up this phase of the sport will find that learning to cast a fly is considerably more difficult than casting with spinning and conventional tackle. And even if you have mastered the technique, you are still handicapped by the inherent limitations involved in casting a weighted line.

Spin fishers and conventional reel anglers talk in terms of casting yards. Fly casters talk in terms of feet. Due to the limitations of their tackle system, fly fishers can never deliver their offerings as far as their spinning and conventional reel counterparts, and this can amount to a dramatic disadvantage when trying to connect with a fish. I have witnessed many instances where beach-bound fly casters put away their fly gear and switched to spinning outfits to reach fish that were out of range with fly tackle. This is an example of where the goal overtakes the emphasis normally placed on the means.

One fall afternoon in the Northeast when striped bass were feeding out beyond our fly-casting range, a friend who did switch gear commented, "Hey, I want to get into these fish." This is nothing to be ashamed of, and the fact that a few of us persisted with our fly gear (fruitlessly, I might add) does not mean that we are purists. I wouldn't even say it's a case of being stubborn. It's simply a matter of choosing to fish by means of a method that gives you the most satisfaction.

Of course, it's possible to circumvent this casting limitation with fly gear if you're fishing from a boat because you can troll the fly. One of my friends who guides in the Northeast has a number of clients who want to catch blues and stripers on fly gear but they can't cast. When I first commented to him about the number of times I've seen his clients trolling flies through the rips, his response was that he was simply trying to accommodate his customers. They wanted to catch fish on fly tackle and were not concerned with distinctions as to how the fly was presented. Similar to the issue of using bait, fly tackle is being used but it is not fly fishing.

Since deviations like these do not involve violations of any formal laws, you may ask, who cares? Here too the discipline of sociology can help provide an answer. As with many rule violations, people who are not involved, not interested, or do not perceive themselves to be affected by the activity generally do not really care if the rule has been breached. In many cases they don't even know that such rules exist. If you come back from vacation and tell your coworkers you caught a wahoo on your fly rod, unless they had an interest in or knowledge of the sport, the distinction between trolling and casting the fly or whether it may have been tipped with bait or scented simply would not be relevant to them. But for those of you who developed an affinity for the sport, there is a strong presumption that such distinctions are important and meaningful because you are participants in this subculture of fly fishing. Regardless of all our other innumerable socio-cultural differences, as fly fishers the manner in which the fish was caught is, as they say, a "big deal" to us.

What we are talking about here is recognition in terms of approval, and this is always socially based. Some other person has to recognize our achievement, but since our social audiences differ, the level of recognition we receive also differs. Friends who have little interest in or knowledge of fishing may congratulate you on your catch, but this response and your reaction to that response is considerably different when the social audience consists of kindred fly fishers. Those who have presented flies to permit or tried to cast a fly to marauding wahoo from a pitching deck know what a tough game we're playing, and because their acknowledgement of our achievement is so meaningful, it serves as a great boost to our sense of pride and self-esteem.

Similar to a common practice among some Northeast fly fishers who simply have their flies drift in a rip current without casting, many folks fishing Baja troll their flies behind a panga. But to be truly fly fishing, you have to actually fly cast, as I'm doing in this photo taken by Dan Blanton down in Loreto.

Unfortunately it is this quest for social recognition that often drives people to circumvent the rules. They know they have cheated, but if others are unaware of this, they receive the sought-after recognition and that's all that matters to them. There are wealthy anglers who cheat in tournaments not for the money, but for the enhanced social status. It is the same reason some anglers seek IGFA records they don't deserve because they didn't play by the rules.

There was an incident years ago where an angler at a lodge we were both staying at was going through the rather tedious process of submitting a fish he caught that morning for an IGFA fly record. I was somewhat suspicious because this person had a checkered reputation in the fly-fishing community. About a month later when I returned to the lodge, I had an opportunity to question the boat captain and mate about the catch. The captain was very excited about the prospect of having a record catch associated with his boat, but at the time he had no knowledge whatsoever of the IGFA or any of its regulations. As I had seen for myself, the fish was caught on a rod, reel, and fly line system that conformed to IGFA specifications. I did not check the leader, so I'm not sure if the tippet that was submitted for review was the same one that was used to catch the fish. In any case the IGFA found that it did conform to the length and break-strength parameters, and the record was eventually granted. Unfortunately the IGFA officials weren't privy to the conversation I had with the captain and mate, who clearly told me the fly was trolled, not cast. At the time, they were still totally unaware that this would have invalidated the record.

In contrast to the situation above where the captain and mate who served as witnesses to the catch were duped, I recall a case where two friends who were very familiar with IGFA fly-fishing regulations refused to be part of a cheating ruse and prevented a bogus record. Many years ago an acquaintance of theirs (now deceased) who owned a fly shop caught an albacore in northern Baja waters that would have ranked as one of the first to be taken on fly tackle, and he was determined to submit it to the IGFA for a record. Unfortunately his tippet did not conform to the specifications, and he was in the process of tying up another one that he made sure would do so. My two friends with whom he shared the boat vigorously protested. His response was that he was only doing it because it would be good for his fly-fishing business. The only reason he didn't go through with this was because these two anglers threatened to write letters exposing his fraud.

At the opposite end of the continuum, there are those rare occasions when the rules can conspire to actually shift the odds in the angler's favor. One day when I was discussing IGFA regulations with Captain Scott Leon, he told me about an incredible incident that took place during a Florida Keys sailfish tournament. The tournament was catch-and-release, and everyone was supposed to fish according to IGFA regulations. The angler who related the story to Scott was an experienced saltwater fly fisher who logged considerable time pursuing billfish. He hooked a small sailfish, about 40 pounds or so, that went absolutely ballistic when it felt the fly hook in the corner of its jaw. It was close to the boat when it struck, and the angler was able to make a few strips of line to the point where the leader's butt section was inside the rod's tip-top. According to IGFA rules, this constitutes a catch. The fish then shook the fly loose and attacked it a second time in the water. The angler managed to stick the fish and once again succeeded in getting the leader to the rod's tip. The sailfish went airborne and dislodged the fly a second time, but it didn't matter because the second sequence of events was also regarded as a legal catch. He had two legal catch-and-releases in less than a minute and won the tournament.

So where does all this lead to regarding the issue of fly-fishing regulations? Well, unlike laws where we are legally obligated to follow the rules within the parameters established by state and federal regulations, we can use fly tackle in just about any manner we choose. The judgment as to whether

Casting is the name of the game, particularly when you play it in salt water. As in any sport, the only way to progress is to practice. Trying to clear this hula-hoop-type loop makes for some fun practice sessions and will significantly sharpen your accuracy skills.

ED JAWOROSKI

or not fly fishers should abide by these rules is relative. Personally, most of the time I fly fish according to the rules, not so much for the possibility of a record, but more so for the personal satisfaction I derive from confronting the challenges imposed by the regulations. When I choose to disregard some of the regulations, it invariably involves the specifications regarding either the class tippet and/or the bite tippet. In terms of the former, there are circumstances where I find it expedient to exceed the IGFA's maximum 20-pound tippet class (there are seven class tippet categories: 2-, 4-, 6-, 8-, 12-, 16-, and 20-pound test). Fishing from a jetty is one of them. Instead of climbing down slippery rocks to release a fish, I'll hand-line it up and to do that I need a fairly heavy leader. Under circumstances like this, trying to conform to the IGFA's tippet classes is simply not a consideration.

Another example dates back to my early encounters with giant jungle tarpon in Costa Rica. The late Bill Barnes owned and operated the famed Casa Mar lodge that boasted some of the world's best tarpon and snook fishing. I was fortunate to fish this area many times over the years. As an added bonus to the incredible fishing, there were opportunities to fish with and learn from some of the sport's greats like Lefty Kreh and the late Harry Kime, both of whom fished there often.

One day was particularly memorable because I fished with Lefty all morning and Harry that afternoon. At the time the maximum IGFA class tippet was 16-pound test, and that's what I was fishing coupled with an IGFA regulation 12-inch length of 80-pound-test bite tippet. Lefty wanted to take some close-up photos, and after two big fish broke me off in the strong current running through the river mouth, he looked at my leader and insisted that I use 40-pound for the class tippet and lengthen the bite tippet to about $2\frac{1}{2}$ feet. I remember him saying in his half-joking manner, "We're here to take photos, not hunt for records." The irony in this is that Lefty was instrumental in formulating the specifications for the IGFA's fly-fishing division.

That afternoon I shared a boat with Harry, who at the time had probably taken more tarpon on fly than anyone. For the last few years of his life, Harry practically lived at Casa Mar and all he fished for were tarpon. I would come into the dining hall and tell him about some of the big snook and machaca I tangled with and he would say, "That's fine, bandito, you fish them." Harry also fished much heavier leaders on these tarpon, and that afternoon when I questioned him about it, he said he wasn't interested in records and he lost fewer flies. Trying to set a record was not on my priority list either, and the following day I switched to heavier leaders and began losing far fewer fish and flies. I was also able to boat and subsequently release these fish in a shorter time frame that hopefully added to their survival rate.

I would like to add that in cases like the above, the advantage in using heavier break-strength tippets has little or nothing to do with any added pressure you can apply to the fish. With fly gear you are seldom able to establish more than 5 pounds of pressure against the fish. Instead, the added benefit lies in the heavier leader's larger diameter that makes it less likely to fail due to the effects of abrasion. Tarpon and snook are prime examples of fish that can wear through a leader like a power sander. In a similar vein, limiting the length of the bite tippet to only 12 inches can be a significant handicap, particularly when fishing billfish and sharks. A fish's bill can easily reach the fragile class tippet and slice it like a razor. If a leader rubs across a shark's skin (which is a continuation of its dentition), the game will also end quickly.

When the rules are scrupulously followed, setting a fly rod record can be quite an accomplishment and is something to be proud of. The downside to this is that some anglers are so preoccupied and driven by this quest that the element of fun falls by the wayside. This brings to mind some early trips to the Florida Keys where I was in the company of a record-driven fly fisher who would disgustedly break off 100-pound-class tarpon because he wanted the bigger specimen (hopefully of record proportions) to take his fly. In most situations I enjoyed his company, but I didn't particularly like fishing with him because all that mattered to him was establishing a record. I remember a puzzled look on his face one day when I told him I was glad that I never felt the need to prematurely break off fish like that.

In conclusion, as far as my personal experiences are concerned and those of countless others I've met over the years, if you choose to commit yourself to fly fishing within the established IGFA guidelines, at least in terms of casting and manipulating offerings specifically designed for that purpose, you are setting the stage for some very satisfying outings on the water. In

For many years trying to coax a permit to take an artificial offering was thought to be well nigh impossible. It is fairly commonplace today, but many anglers have spent considerable sums pursuing permit on fly. Regardless of size, they are akin to the Holy Grail for fly fishers plying their sport on tropical flats. Corbett Davis Jr. nailed this one in Belize.

the end it's all about fond memories, and you don't need a certificate on the wall to prove it.

Attitude Is Everything

When pursuing fish there's a good deal of truth to the old adage "Timing is everything." But in terms of getting the most enjoyment from your fly-fishing outings, perhaps we can modify that to read "Attitude is everything." Two areas that bear mentioning in this respect are one's ego and the judgments we make about what species are worthy of our fly-fishing efforts.

As a male I take no pleasure in writing this, but the instances I've witnessed where attempts to satisfy one's ego needs have adversely affected the fishing experience have been overwhelmingly confined to anglers of my gender. I've found this especially true when teaching folks to cast. I've repeated this many times: I find women generally to be better students. They tend to be more receptive to what you are trying to impart, but most important of all, they are not burdened with the testosterone-driven compulsion to make distance the sole criterion of their casting ability. In so many cases where I've given lessons to couples, the woman ends up casting more effectively than her male companion. And in cases where you offer unsolicited help, unlike men, women seldom decline the opportunity to improve their casting.

I recall a trip to the Yucatan some time ago that serves as a good example of how our attitudes affect our fishing experiences. Two of the guests at the lodge that week were a husband-and-wife couple who were both new to the sport. Despite the inexperience the husband made it abundantly clear that his sole objective was to catch a permit on fly. He obviously had been told or read somewhere that they represent the Holy Grail of the flats. The lodge owner asked me to accompany them one day because their guide was new and spoke very little English, and the couple didn't know any Spanish.

The husband blew his first two opportunities at permit that morning simply because he couldn't cast the required distance. We took a break for lunch and as judiciously as possible I asked him if I could help him "fine-tune" his casting (major overhaul was more like it). He politely declined and felt his casting was fine, implying that the guide could have placed him in a more favorable position. His wife, however, jumped at the invitation and readily admitted that she needed the instruction. It didn't take long before she started making relatively effortless casts with nice, tight loops. She didn't get a permit but managed two nice snook and was thrilled by the experience. The husband caught three or four jacks but wasn't satisfied because he didn't get his permit. As I recall only three were taken that entire week.

That same evening after dinner, I overheard the husband speaking with the owner where he began criticizing the guide's performance. He complained that the guide didn't position him close enough to the permit and consequently he was never able to get off a decent cast to the fish. Shortly afterward I was able to get with the owner and told him there was nothing wrong with the guide, and that in the guide's judgment if he poled us any closer, the permit would have spooked. I don't know whether the couple still fly fishes; if so, I hope the husband's ego needs have receded to the point where he's receptive to some badly needed casting instruction.

The husband's obsession with catching a permit illustrates a second attitudinal posture that can cast a pall on one's fishing experience. This was their first saltwater trip, and he already had the expectation that he was going to catch a prize permit. That's closely akin to a rookie pitcher expecting to throw a shutout his first time on the mound. It's within the realm of possibility, but in reality the odds are pretty slim. There was one very accomplished angler at the lodge that week who told this fellow he had spent considerable sums on taking trips like this but had still not yet connected with a permit. This guy did not want to hear it.

Unquestionably taking a permit on fly is a worthy accomplishment, and there is certainly nothing wrong with this fellow's determination to accomplish this feat. However, what I found troubling was the way in which he denigrated species like the snapper and jacks he caught. The latter he tended to regard as trash fish even though some of the ones he landed exceeded the double-digit mark. The lodge owner tried to assure him that pound for pound the jacks pulled harder than any permit, but this didn't console him for his failure to connect with the latter.

His high regard for permit and his disparagement for these other species are obviously two very different mindsets, yet they share the same origin. They are both the products of social definition. It is nonsense to think that a fish has some innate value. Instead, it is the community of anglers who render the declaration as to a fish's worth. If a fish is noble or prized, it is only because we say it is so. Quite naturally when people are driven to fishing to eat or sell their catch, the principal determination of a fish's worth is its value as table fare, but this too is infused with a good deal of subjectivity. For example, some like the taste of mackerel, others detest it.

In the realm of sport, a fish's worth tends to be based on qualities we deem important aside from its consideration as a food source. Like recreational fishers in general, as fly fishers we tend to evaluate a fish's status in terms of two factors: how difficult it is to catch and the degree of resistance it affords once it's hooked. In terms of the first factor, prior to a consideration of the challenge involved in enticing a fish to take a fly is the question of availability. Regardless of how eager a fish may be to accept an artificial offering, if the fish is not abundant or easily accessed, the chances of hooking one are greatly reduced.

This brings us to the notion of scarcity and the economic principle of supply and demand. Our everyday world is replete with examples of how scarcity can elevate the value of a commodity. In the sport-fishing realm, we can see this illustrated in comparing the catch value of the two species we mentioned above, the permit and the jack. Permit are more locale-specific than jacks, and compared to the latter they are nowhere near as abundant or as easily accessed by the rank-and-file angler. True, they are far more difficult to entice with flies than jacks, and that has a great deal to do with their prized status. But so does the fact that they have an exotic quality, because unlike jacks they are not readily available to most anglers.

On the other side of the scale, an abundance of fish that are within easy reach of many anglers can slip into a syndrome summarized in the ancient adage "Familiarity breeds contempt." A classic example is the bonito fishery in my old hometown of Redondo Beach, California. Up until the mid-1980s bonito were plentiful off the Southern California coast, and Redondo Beach's King Harbor boasted a world-class fishery for this junior member of the tuna clan. The live-bait barges anchored in the harbor in conjunction with a

The rock-dwelling cabrilla makes for excellent table fare, but that's a consideration entirely different from its sporting qualities. They don't jump like dorado or boast roosterfish-like speed, but as Brandon Powers can testify, they pull hard and can pose quite a challenge trying to wrench them from their rocky habitat.

A small Baja roosterfish, one of 21 taken in one day by Brandon Powers, all on regulation fly tackle.

Left: For anglers in Southern California, the white sea bass is a highly prized game fish. Most are taken on conventional gear with live bait. If you want to maximize the sporting qualities of this fish, try challenging them on regulation fly-fishing tackle.
Right: Though disparaged by some, jacks like this are great fun on fly gear. They are one of the strongest fighting fish you'll encounter on any tackle.

They are often found in the same locales and exhibit basically the same sporting qualities, but for some reason drum like the one pictured have not garnered the same notoriety as redfish. I would never pass up the opportunity to present a fly to one.

warmwater outflow from the Edison plant played a major role in attracting large schools of these "silver bullets." There were times when I stood atop the breakwater and observed schools of fish that took a full five minutes to swim by. My home was only five minutes from the harbor, and there was one year where I logged over 300 days on the breakwater tossing flies to the "bones." One well-traveled friend with whom I shared this horn of plenty commented that fly fishers would spend hundreds of dollars to stand on the rocks with us and cast to these great game fish.

We cherished and respected this fishery, but not everyone in the Southern California sport-fishing community shared our sentiments. Despite their legendary fighting quality, the bonito's relative abundance had a lot to do with the fact that they were unappreciated by a sizable contingent of anglers. Regulars on the party boat circuit cursed them when they intercepted baits and lures intended for more highly prized species like bluefin tuna and yellowtail, and anglers fishing the harbor saw nothing wrong in filling the parking lot trash bins with bonito they recently caught. However, anglers who lived in areas where bonito were scarce or nonexistent had a great deal more respect for these fish. Fly-fishing clubs from places like central California and Arizona held annual group outings in King Harbor to partake in what they considered a fabulous fishery. Today the fishery is only a shadow of what it once was, and the current generation of anglers would relish the opportunity to sample the kind of action we were privileged to experience in the past.

This relationship between a species' abundance and its assigned value as a game fish may help explain the comparatively low sporting status typically accorded fish like East Coast bluefish, jack crevalle, and oceanic skipjack, to name a few. Guides frequently complain about how some of their clients disavow fish like this because it makes their job of providing a rewarding experience on the water all the more difficult. But many times the guides themselves perpetuate the problem by openly displaying their dissatisfaction when for whatever reason clients fail to connect with what they consider to be the "right" fish. Statements like "We only got blues today," "The damn jacks were everywhere," or "We couldn't get a fly past the skippies" are the sort of comments that reinforce negative attitudes about game fish with sporting credentials that otherwise could provide a great deal of enjoyment to the angling public.

For my part I prefer to abide by a philosophy I learned a long time ago from a fly fisher I encountered on a remote stretch of beach in Baja. I never got his name but asked how he was doing and vividly recall what he said: "I caught a rooster yesterday and hope some show today, but I'm having a lot of fun with these cabrilla and needlefish. Anything that goes for my fly and straightens my leader, I'll throw a cast to."

2 The Saltwater Realm

The surf is a magical realm because you are standing at the ocean's doorstep. And as is true in many locales, low-light conditions are often the best time to fish.

Traditionally most anglers started their fly-fishing careers in fresh water. This is still largely the case today; however, with the upsurge of interest in saltwater fly fishing, an increasing number of fly fishers are making their initial entrée into the sport in some sort of marine environment, ranging all the way from tidal flats to the high seas. I fall into the latter case.

Particularly where children are involved, the choice of where to fish is primarily governed by accessibility and affordability. Fortunately I grew up close to salt water in the

15

form of Long Island Sound and had uncles who were fond of renting skiffs for a day on the water. They also liked to fish for flounder, fluke, blackfish, and porgies, all of which were plentiful at the time. Using simple hand lines it was possible for two anglers to fill a bushel basket full of flounder in a couple of hours. I played most sports and frolicked in the winter's snows, but always longed for spring when we could start making our first trips on the sound. The gear was simple, but the fun quotient never ebbed. Even when I eventually acquired a bait-casting outfit as a present, I often resorted to using a hand line because I loved the sensation of the strike being transmitted directly to my hands.

This is one of the principal factors that drew me to fly fishing. Throughout the years I've had great fun using all kinds gear ranging from ultralight spinning to big-game blue-water tackle, but fly gear is my favorite mode and since the mid-1980s it is the only way I choose fish. I mentioned this to Rod Harrison, a great Aussie angler who is a master with all tackle modes, and his now-classic response was, "Mate, that's because fly fishing is fishing with a hand line that you can cast."

While there is a great deal of crossover between fresh- and saltwater fly fishing in terms of both tackle and technique, in many respects fly fishing in salt water is a world unto itself. The sheer vastness and variety of locales presents a near-limitless array of opportunities and challenges. In addition to the formidable conditions often encountered in this environment, the species you fish for in salt water are typically stronger, swifter, and larger than their freshwater counterparts. There is some truth to a saying often uttered in half-jest that the only time freshwater anglers see their backing is when they wind it on the reel for the first time. This is not to imply that all saltwater game fish are line burners, but most pull hard and put forth a dogged resistance that's especially intensified with fly gear.

There are some freshwater buffs, particularly dry-fly aficionados targeting trout, who tend to hold saltwater species in low regard because they mistakenly believe these fish are always willing to eat almost anything put in front of them. On the contrary, they can be every bit as selective as super-finicky trout in the offerings they choose to strike. Try persuading a permit with a picture-perfect presentation and the word *refusal* will take on a more poignant meaning. But when you do connect, unlike many freshwater scenarios where the take is everything, with most saltwater game fish the contest is just beginning. Getting locked in a tug-of-war with a member of the tuna clan, trying to put the brakes on an amberjack heading for a sunken wreck, the sensation of a bluefish attacking a popper, and watching a bonefish make a blistering run across a flat in ankle-deep water are the kind of encounters that draw more and more fly fishers to the saltwater realm.

There is also the factor of accessibility. A substantial portion of the US population lives within easy commuting distance to the Pacific, the Gulf, or the Atlantic coasts and vast stretches of coastline are open to the public. This makes launching trailer boats and a host of personal watercraft like kayaks and kick boats or wading the beaches, bays, and estuaries practical choices for those who want to venture into salt water to fly fish. In the '70s I owned center-console skiffs both in the Northeast and when I relocated back to Southern California. I've also fished from kayaks, kick boats, and float tubes (not recommended). Presently a great deal of my saltwater fly fishing is by means of wading.

Considering both the quality of the fishery along with minimal expense and hassle, walking the shoreline ranks as a very desirable way to enter the saltwater fly-fishing realm. The variety of species you can expect to take on flies from shore could easily fill a marine biology text. Here's a brief overview of what I've experienced: In my home waters of Southern California, the major surf species are barred perch, yellowfin croaker, corbina, and halibut. Crossing the border into Baja, particularly on the Sea of Cortez side, the game fish lineup takes on major-league dimensions. Cabrilla, jacks, pompano, large needlefish, sierra mackerel, and even the prized roosterfish can all be taken from the beach. Along the southwest Texas coast, there are redfish, sea trout, and challenging sheepshead. On Florida's southwest coastline, including Naples and the beautiful stretches of beach on Sanibel, Captiva, and Marco Islands, you'll find snook, jacks, pompano, and reds.

Whenever possible my favorite method of fishing the beach is to sight-fish. Fortunately in Southern California I'm able to do this from spring to early fall for the ultra-finicky corbina. I've found these more difficult to entice with flies than wary permit. Maybe it's an instance of the "grass is always greener" syndrome, but high on my list of shore-bound sight-fishing is the snook fishery in southwest Florida. Not long ago while wading shin deep in windowpane-clear water at Naples Beach, I noticed a dark shape out of the corner of my eye. At first I thought it was a piece of wood. I turned to get a better look, and the shape suddenly bolted past me. I was so startled that I almost lost my balance. My surprise was quickly transformed into frustration as I saw a snook the size of my lower leg swim out to deeper water. Thinking back on it, similar to a tactic I often employ when stalking corbina, I probably would have fared better walking a little farther up on the beach and not getting my feet wet. That's something to consider whenever you're wading a clear-water beach.

If you want to experience the most dramatic signs of fish marauding along the coastline, hit the beaches in the Northeast during the fall season. Schools are often mixed and there can be striped bass, bluefish, and false albacore all tearing into terrified pods of baitfish they've herded into the beachfront.

Here I am sight-fishing corbina that are swimming close to where the water laps the shoreline. To avoid spooking them, I'm staying back on the wet sand.

The action can be absolute mayhem, as the fish are prone to pop up and down along different sections of shoreline, and normally the way my luck runs, the feeding spree always seems to be happening a fair distance from where I'm wading. Running down the beach trying to get into position while

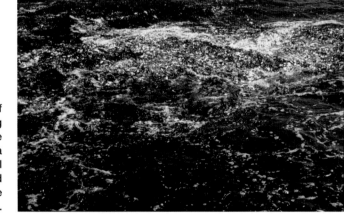

This is a pod of baitfish being driven to the surface by a mixed school of bluefish and stripers off Rhode Island in the fall.

When fly fishing salt water you can find yourself in some incredibly diverse environments. Fishing along some of the islands in Baja's Sea of Cortez can seem like a desert oasis.

In Baja the terrain can be as formidable as the critters you battle in its fish-rich waters.

wearing chest-high waders can be every bit as taxing as the final stages of a runner's marathon.

When you fish salt water, especially from a shoreline, you have to pay particular attention to the tides. In case you may have forgotten, here is brief refresher on the subject: Tides are the result of the gravitational pull of the moon and sun. Twice each month when both planets are in straight alignment relative to Earth, there is maximum gravitational effect that results in unusually high and low tides. These are referred to as spring tides, and they occur during the new and full moon. The opposite of this effect where the sun and moon are at right angles to each other produces minimal tidal flow known as neap tides. These occur during the first- and third-quarter moon phases. Both tidal effects occur in weekly cycles, so a week of spring tides is followed by a week of neap tides and so on throughout the year. If you experienced some outstanding fishing at "Somewhere Point" and returned to the same spot one week later, you would encounter a totally different set of tidal conditions.

Now, while it's possible to catch fish throughout the tidal cycle, there are definitely periods that are consistently more productive than others. Generally, for any stretch of beach you're fishing, the best action will occur during periods of maximum tidal movement. Moving water pushes, pulls, tumbles, and disperses all manner of fish food items from crabs to worms to baitfish. Fish tune into these periods when food sources are more readily available and feed accordingly.

Translating into tidal phases, this means that you will generally experience the best fishing during incoming and outing tides. Experience will teach you which of the tidal phases produces best for the particular places you fish. The period between the two where there is minimal water movement is called the slack tide or slack water. Since the fish probably won't be doing much feeding, this is usually a good time to take a break.

Of course, no one rod, reel, and line combination can do it all, but by far most inshore and coastal fishing can be handled with 6- to 9-weight outfits (though the fly line weight differs dramatically, these numerical weight designations apply to both single- and doubled-handed rods). Perhaps the most versatile would be an 8-weight single-handed outfit. I prefer shooting heads (we will look at this in more detail) for most coastal applications and particularly when fishing the beach because they enable you to change lines quickly. Except for relatively calm, shallow water (Long Island Sound and the southwest Florida beaches are good examples) where I normally use a weight-forward floating line, intermediate and fast-sinking heads are ideal choices for the beach. As we'll see, some type of line management device is an absolute must.

This photo of one of my favorite surf spots on Silver Strand Beach in Coronado, California, was taken during a period of maximum tidal movement.

Using Fly Gear in Salt Water

When you are fishing salt water, you're talking maintenance, and this will include every piece of equipment you bring into play from watercraft to fly gear. I'll leave watercraft maintenance to others but just want to emphasize from the safety standpoint alone, you want anything that is carrying you out on the water to be in tip-top condition. It can't get any simpler than a float tube (which I do not recommend for open-water saltwater fishing), but I had one fail and had to make an arduous and dangerous swim to get back on solid ground.

To get the most out of your fishing experience, you also want all your tackle components to be in proper working order. Not too long ago Southern California had a banner year for yellowfin tuna, dorado, and yellowtail. Unfortunately an abundance of game fish of this fighting caliber is often accompanied by a wave of malfunctioning or broken tackle. Naturally some failures are simply unavoidable and can be chalked up to plain old bad luck

Zane Grey referred to the mako as the aristocrat of sharks. Here one goes airborne offshore from San Diego. Be prepared to sacrifice some flies when you fish these "grinners."

CAPTAIN SCOTT LEON

and the fact that nothing can be expected to last forever. In fly fishing, leaders and flies are good examples. Even under normal conditions these two items usually do not enjoy long-term longevity. Today most fly hooks designed for salt water are rust resistant and pre-sharpened, but they can be dulled. For that reason I always carry a file with me. Rising's Diamond File is a good choice because it is small and has grooves for easy touch-up work.

Tooth-studded species like barracuda, bluefish, sharks, and wahoo can easily tear up flies. Without a wire bite tippet (this will be covered in the chapter on knots), you would be lucky to even get your fly back. Species like snook and tarpon do not have cutting teeth but can quickly reduce a section of monofilament to shreds. Sometimes even after contacting one fish with the leader still intact, a change may be in order. In the days when I fished big yellowfin tuna on conventional tackle on long-range boats, it was standard practice to completely strip all the monofilament line off the reel after landing a big fish (with the advent of braided lines, this is no longer necessary). The reason was that during the struggle the monofilament line could have been stressed to its limit, and to avoid any premature breakage with another fish, the safest course was simply to spool on fresh line.

After a prolonged struggle with a big fish, a fly leader can also be subject to the same type of stress, so even though there may be no signs of abrasion or wear, I take the precaution of putting on a new leader (with pre-tied leaders and loop-to-loop connections, leader changes are quick and easy to make). The leader is a critical link between you and the fish, so if there are any doubts about its integrity, the simple rule of thumb is to change it. If you purchase your monofilament leader material in bulk spools, you can expect it to last for many years, but do not store it where it's exposed to direct sunlight.

Under normal usage fly lines have a life expectancy far longer than leaders, but this can be shortened considerably if you do things like spill gasoline on the line or have it roll under your shoes, causing it to rub over an abrasive surface like some nonskid boat decks. All matter of fishing situations can cause problems. I've had bluefish bite a fly line that was pulled through the water when I was hooked to one of their brethren. Apparently the fish was attracted to the rooster-tail effect of the line slicing through the surface. If you fish for species that are structure oriented, you can expect similar mishaps. Snook and striped bass have ruined lines that were dragged across barnacle-encrusted dock pilings and channel markers. Tarpon and tuna diving under a boat pulling the line over the keel will inflict similar damage. Some of these mishaps can also occur in fresh water, but normally a saltwater environment is considerably harsher.

Every time I fish the salt I make it a practice to strip the fly line off the reel and rinse it with fresh water. I can't say this actually contributes to the line's longevity, but it does prevent the buildup of salt crystals and I find the line shoots more smoothly through the guides when it's clean. I also rinse off the rod and reel.

For years it's been standard practice to carry numerous flies and leaders, but particularly among those who fish the salt, where feasible (fishing from a boat, for example) an increasing number of anglers are finding it prudent to have more than one rod and reel on hand. These two items are the most durable part of our equipment system. They are also the most expensive, but to offset that cost, barring accidents and improper use, they can be expected to last indefinitely.

Reels are more mechanically complex than rods, but due to the nature of their construction, they tend to be more durable. That said, I've seen the spool spread on some very expensive models under the strain of big tuna. I dropped one top-dollar model on the garage floor and bent the frame. However, accidents like this aside, you can normally expect reels to last a very long time. Again, for those fished in salt water, it's good practice to give them a freshwater rinse and some periodic lubrication, and back off on the drag mechanism. I've fished many of my reels in salt water for over 30 years and have never experienced a problem. Most have suffered a lot of scratches, but they continue to function flawlessly.

As with most products in this sport, you have a great deal to choose from when selecting a reel for saltwater fly fishing. Two major options to consider are whether to opt for a direct drive versus an anti-reverse, and whether the reel should be right- or left-hand wind (most models feature pop-off spools

Snook and tarpon are among the top favorites in Florida's stellar game fish lineup, and they don't have to be monster size to make for a lot of fun on fly gear. These two specimens were taken in Naples Bay.

Left: King mackerel are not normally associated with this sport, but when you can locate them, they will usually readily take a fly. Captain Roan Zumfelde primarily fishes inshore along Florida's southwest coast, but when game fish like these kings show up only a few miles offshore, he's right on them.

Below left: Though they characteristically attack flies with a savage strike and fight like an enraged pit bull, in many quarters bluefish are undeservedly regarded as second-class game fish.

Below right: Though not as fierce as their tropical cousins, Southern California barracuda do sport dentures—not the type that could sever a finger, but certainly sharp enough to cut through light monofilament tippets. Since wire bite tippets tend to turn them off, I try to circumvent their teeth by using flies with long-shank hooks.

and can be easily converted to left- or right-hand wind). The majority of fly reels are direct drive, meaning that the handle will spin backwards as line is being pulled from the spool. This is my personal preference. Because it is direct drive, when you crank on the handle there is absolutely no line slippage, but you do have to learn to be careful of the rapidly spinning handle when a strong fish decides to make a run for it.

To help deal with this, most fly reels designed for salt water feature an exposed spool rim. This makes it possible to apply pressure with your fingers or the palm of your hand, staying clear of the spinning handle. The exposed spool rim is a great fish-fighting tool because it enables you to immediately apply additional pressure or back off as needed. No mechanical drag system can react as quickly as palming the spool in this manner. When I battle fish large or small, the reel's drag mechanism plays only a minor role. I have it set relatively light so I can pull line out with little effort. If more resistance is needed, I apply it to the exposed spool rim. However, when a fish suddenly bolts forward or dives below, I can instantly react and back off, eliminating the prospect of broken tippets.

The question of right- or left-hand wind should be a no-brainer, but there are some who argue the issue. Wind with your dominant hand. For most folks this means using their right hand. If you cannot turn a reel handle as effectively with your left hand, use your right—it's that simple. The argument for a right-handed caster selecting left-hand wind is that you don't have to switch hands to perform a casting function and winding the reel handle, but there is so little effort in doing so that it becomes a nonissue. Many times a fish will turn and suddenly run toward you. When this happens you want to retrieve line as quickly as possible, and unless you are ambidextrous, you can only do so with your dominant hand.

Like it or not, rods are considerably more fragile. I guess you could make a rod that is practically unbreakable, but then it wouldn't be fishable. When you think about it, we ask two very critical functions of our rods: They have to cast, and they must be able to fight fish. In many respects these two requirements oppose one another, and depending on the type of fishing you're involved in, one function may be more important than the other. For example, a rod designated as a boat rod has one primary function: to fight fish. That rod is seldom if ever used for casting, so the rod's performance in that regard is not really a consideration in its design and construction. That is the reason manufacturers offer so many rod models and styles.

As far as maintenance is concerned, it couldn't be simpler. With every new rod before I ever fish it I apply a little marine-grade grease to the reel seat grooves. This way the screw-type rings are always easy to tighten and loosen, even for those like myself with arthritic fingers. After saltwater use

Even when you think everything is fine, mishaps can still occur. Here my fly rod broke during battle with a Costa Rican tarpon. I had taken many 100-pound-plus tarpon on this stick, so I doubt there was a manufacturing defect. Instead, after being banged around for so long the rod probably developed a fissure that caused it to finally give way.

I rinse the rod off with fresh water. If you store the rod in a cloth sock, be sure it is thoroughly dry before doing so, otherwise mildew can develop.

Any rod manufacturer will tell you that breakage is due far more to accidents and angler error than to defects in their construction. You could write a book describing the accidents that befall rods. Let's take a look here at some instances of angler error. Particularly where fly rods are concerned, casting and fish fighting are two areas where mistakes are commonly made that could result in rod breakage. If you make a poor cast with a weighted fly (one that has dumbbell or bead-chain eyes, for example) and strike the rod with it causing a crack or fissure, the rod will more than likely fracture at some point. This may not happen immediately, but with continued use the fissure can become more pronounced until a critical point is reached and the rod finally breaks. The same thing can happen when a rod is constantly banged around in a boat or car. A small crack may be created that gets worse over time, and then the rod breaks seemingly for no apparent reason.

Looks can be deceiving. To the uninitiated it may appear that the angler plucked this fish from the water. Instead, the tarpon has gone airborne. When a big fish like this jumps, the angler should immediately react by lowering the rod to create cushioning slack in the line.

CAPTAIN SCOTT LEON

Many big-game saltwater fly sticks have what are referred to as fighting foregrips placed several inches above the primary grip. It's advisable to avoid placing your rod hand higher than the foregrip. Doing so is referred to as high-sticking.

Contrary to popular belief and practice, rods are not designed to bend like a horseshoe. It's a foolish move to bend a rod like this, and it's also an instance of poor fish-fighting technique. When a bend begins to form above a 45-degree angle, the rod's pulling power is greatly diminished. You can easily demonstrate this for yourself by holding the end of a leader while someone else bends the rod at increasingly higher angles. You will feel the least amount of resistance when the rod is bent in a nearly vertical position. This is also a position where the rod is most likely to break.

A second instance of inefficient technique borrows a term from hockey and is referred to as high-sticking the rod. In hockey you're hit with a foul. In fishing this move can result in a broken rod. Positioning your hand up above the rod grip alters the rod's fulcrum point. The result is that instead of the bend forming from the butt, which is the strongest part of the rod, it starts to form in the upper portion of the rod, which is the weaker section. When you pull back like this, regardless of the rod, there is a good chance the tip section will fail.

Even when the fish is properly fought, a great deal of rod breakage occurs in the stage where the fish is close at hand, ready to be landed. Too often when the leader is grabbed, a radical bend is created in the rod's tip section. You can easily remedy this situation by making sure there is enough line outside the rod tip to where it can be grasped without putting a dangerous bend in the rod's tip section.

There may be considerable nostalgia for the gear that our forebears used, but there is no denying that today's tackle is far more efficient and user-friendly. Taking a few precautions will go a long way in insuring its longevity.

Play It Safe

Even if you plan to fish your home waters, it's always prudent to get advance weather notifications. Any time you venture into or on the water, particularly salt water, always bear in mind that you are dealing with an unforgiving environment.

If you plan to fish from a boat or personal watercraft, get proper instruction before your maiden voyage. With any personal watercraft self-propelled with fins, paddles, or oars, be especially mindful of two factors: your physical limitations and the effects of wind and current. The excursion can take on an entirely different tone if you find yourself having to work against the latter two elements to get back to your launch area.

Captain Scott Leon with a juvenile-size yellowtail referred to by the locals as a "firecracker." The nickname says a lot about their fighting qualities. They will test your tackle to the max.

With larger powered watercraft, despite some ruffled feelings, I've made it a practice to turn down boat trips in cases where I felt the person who would be skippering the vessel wasn't qualified to do so. In contrast, I have no problem running 35 miles or so offshore in an 18-foot skiff with someone like my buddy John Loo, who has decades of experience behind him. Not only are his seamanship skills exemplary, he has practically every small-craft emergency device you can buy on board and is totally familiar with their use. I feel the same way hitting the open ocean with my buddy Captain Scott Leon. Scott was a Navy Seal and trained in many of the locales we now fish together. You couldn't ask for better background experience for operating a boat on the ocean.

Exercising due caution is not limited to operating watercraft. The simple act of walking a beach at the water's edge can be treacherous if you're not paying attention to surf conditions. There are tragic illustrations of this on San Francisco beaches where people who were walking their dog were swept off the beach and drowned by an unexpected wave. When fishing an open beachfront, I take a few minutes to study the wave patterns before wading out and never venture deeper than my knees. With wave action the water may only be at your ankles and seconds later it can be waist deep. Take small steps, and though it can be difficult to do in the surf, try to shuffle your feet along the bottom. Moving slowly, edging your way along, will help prevent you from suddenly stepping into a bottom depression you weren't aware of.

Also, in areas where they are common, the shuffle might save you from stepping on a stingray. My days of fishing barefoot off the beach are over. I've done so all my life, but not long ago within a span of three months I got hit twice off San Diego beaches. The first time I was struck on my left heel. The pain was sharp and intense, and I thought at first I may have stepped on something like a broken clamshell. But as the minutes ticked by and the pain intensified, I was sure it had to be ray. A few hours later this was confirmed in the doctor's office, where he opened the small wound and removed a barb. The second incident was on my left toe. This time I made my way to a lifeguard station, where I was able to soak my foot in hot water. The relief was instantaneous. Apparently the hot water (as hot as you can tolerate) helps break down the bacteria.

One of the most ray-infested areas I've ever fished is Laguna Madre in the Texas Gulf. I was fishing with a guide in a skiff and didn't anticipate having

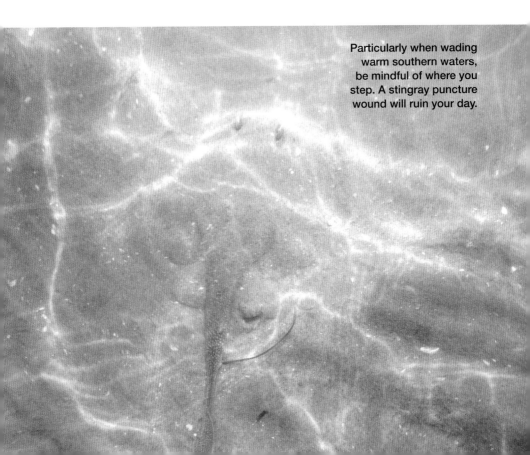

Particularly when wading warm southern waters, be mindful of where you step. A stingray puncture wound will ruin your day.

"Jetty jockey" is an East Coast term for anglers who like to rock hop. Here I'm perched on a rock wall in San Diego Bay, but the same safety precautions should be followed whenever and wherever you're on the rocks.

to get out and wade. In the one spot he took me to do so, the stingrays looked like base pads on a ball field and they were everywhere. I asked my guide about foot protection, and he said he never had a problem as long as he shuffled his feet. I knew all about this but still wished I had something on my feet. This was made worse by the fact that a number of times when I spotted and stalked a good-size sea trout or redfish, I often forgot to shuffle and didn't pay close attention to where I was walking. Not long after I returned home, the guide e-mailed me and wrote that a ray finally nailed him. It sidelined him for about eight weeks.

The obvious lesson to be learned from this is that wearing proper footwear can prevent most of these mishaps. Two wading shoes I wear and can highly recommend are ones offered by Patagonia and Simms. Both resemble high-top tennis shoes. They feature thick, nonslip soles; the material on the uppers provides good ankle support; and they lace up. Dive booties can used but most have zipper fasteners, and when inundated with sand, they can easily jam.

Proper footwear is also critical if you're fishing off rocks or a jetty.

One of the worst ways to go, and unfortunately I've seen this time and again, is to venture out wearing flip-flops. If the bottom of your foot gets wet, it will slip sideways in the flip-flop and you could injure your ankle or fall. They offer no ankle support or toe protection, and the soles are usually not designed to be nonslip. If your feet were tough enough, you would be better off barefoot.

Some rock surfaces can be as slick as greased bowling balls, and without soles specially designed to grip, you are asking for trouble. Jumping from rock to rock is definitely out of the question if you have any balance or orthopedic issues. In the event you take a fall and are lucky enough to escape with a minor bruise, do not assume all is well. Rock outcroppings and jetties can be encrusted with all kinds of bacterial agents as a result of bird and rat droppings. If not cleaned and treated properly, broken skin can quickly become infected.

The best rule of thumb from a safety standpoint is that if you are not sure of where you are stepping, don't go there. On many break walls and jetties, the rocks look like they are firmly in place, but some are piled loosely and if you step on one you can easily lose your balance. There's no fish worth an injury.

When you have a prize like this mako shark close to the boat, be sure to have enough line outside the rod tip so the fish can be safely handled.

3 Preparing for the Encounter

CAPTAIN JOE BLADOS

This is the kind of scenario saltwater fly fishers dream about: predator game fish attacking a school of baitfish within easy casting distance of where you are situated. In this photo it's albies chasing rain bait off the north shore of Long Island. As thrilling as this scene is, it will all go for naught if you're not prepared for the encounter.

"Timing is everything," exclaimed my exuberant friend, who couldn't wait to tell me about the fabulous deal he made on a custom 52-foot sport fisher. He had just come in from an offshore trip and was gathering up his gear when he heard what sounded like a marital spat between a couple who were standing alongside this beautiful yacht berthed a couple of docks down from his charter. The dock master told my friend the couple were novice boaters

34

who spent an unplanned night on the ocean and had to be towed back to the marina. It was the yacht's maiden voyage, but apparently what amounted to a minor fuel problem left them stranded about 45 miles southwest of San Diego harbor. The lady wanted no more boating adventures and insisted that her husband divest himself of the craft as soon as possible. My friend heard this, and jokingly offered to take it off their hands for what he considered to be a ridiculous price. The lady said, "You bought yourself a boat." Her husband protested but to no avail, and my friend acquired the vessel for almost half its original selling price.

Certainly my friend's good fortune is a classic example of "timing is everything" or the equally familiar "being in the right place at the right time." These are commonplace expressions, and one often hears them bandied about in fishing circles to account for an angler's success. But like most popular truisms, on their face they do not tell the whole story. In my friend's case, good fortune notwithstanding, he had to have the wherewithal to make the purchase and this involved a great deal more than simple timing. Years of hard work and careful money management resulted in his having the funds on hand to make this opportune purchase. And so it is with fishing. Timing is important, and we all dream about the occasions when fish are abundant and willing recipients of offerings tossed their way. However, even under these most favorable conditions, if an angler is ill prepared, success will prove elusive.

Surprisingly, in the many instructional books and magazine articles devoted to fly-fishing techniques and tackle, one topic that seems to receive only scant attention is the visibility factor. When I was young I did a lot of blue-water fishing in Southern California and Baja, both recreational and commercial. Still living at home with my parents, I wasn't confronted with the harsh reality of trying to make a living off what I caught, and it was a lot of fun being out on the water even when I had work responsibilities. Catching is the name of the game when fishing for profit, and this includes sport-fishing operations with paying customers. Everything is geared to maximize the catch rate, and many of the techniques I learned on the commercial boats served me well when fishing was purely recreational.

For example, on the offshore grounds one of the standard orders issued to someone who was about to pull lookout duty on the boat's tuna tower was to "keep your eyeballs on." As I gradually learned, being on the alert for fish activity involves considerably more than simply keeping a sharp eye. You must be prepared, and in the case of spotting fish it involves a dual consideration of knowing how to look and what to look for, part of a process often referred to as "reading the water" whereby one learns to interpret the vast array of signs nature presents us. This is not a speed-reading exercise. It

Bonefishing in skinny water is flats fishing in its classic form. It's a totally visual game, and you must constantly scan the surface for telltale signs. From a distance all you might see is the tip of the caudal fin on this tailing bonefish.

takes repeated practice and experience. Much of what I learned in this respect stems from my fishing experience in salt water, but it applies equally as well to freshwater environments.

In terms of "how to look," the first consideration is appropriate eyewear. Safety is a foremost consideration and for that reason alone fly fishers should wear glasses any time they pick up a rod to cast, regardless if they are needed to improve vision. Hooks are not the only danger. I witnessed two instances at fly-fishing shows where a bystander suffered injury from the tag end of a leader striking their eye. Even when you only may be observing, it's a good idea to wear glasses any time you're in close proximity to someone who is casting.

Polarized glasses will shield your eyes from flying objects as well as the sun's harmful rays, but they serve an additional function because they cut through surface glare and make it possible to more clearly distinguish objects in the water. A great way to test the effectiveness of polarized lenses is to try looking at an object in the water first with a pair of non-polarized glasses and then with a polarized pair. You will immediately detect a marked difference. The object will be more clearly visible with the polarized glasses, and for that reason alone in daylight conditions I would never fish without a pair. In terms of blocking light rays, they function like louvers on venetian blinds and only admit those rays that are on a horizontal plane. If you tilt your head to the side while wearing a pair, you'll be able to see the effect.

While the choice between polarized and non-polarized glasses is obvious, selecting a particular shade or tint that best suits the water environment you'll be fishing is a little more involved. If you have to limit yourself to one pair, try to select a color that is best suited to the type of fishing you do most. For example, if most of your fishing takes place in clear, shallow water, amber-tinted lenses are probably the best choice. But be advised that different manufacturers label what I am referring to as amber with a variety of different designations such as brown, tan, and even bronze. What these tints all have in common is that they are designed to enhance contrast and make it easier to see fish in shallow water.

For saltwater fly fishers, bonefish would most likely lead the list of species most sought after when sight-fishing in shallow water. They have a bluish tint and amber lenses block the blue wavelength, giving the fish more contrast against the bottom background. But what complicates matters is the fact that not all flats are the same. They exhibit different bottom compositions that give rise to different hues in the color spectrum, with the result that one shade of amber may work better in some places and not as well in others. Thus it's been my experience that a pair of glasses I used in areas like the Bahamas with broad expanses of sandy bottom were not as effective in trying to pick out bonefish on shallow-water flats in Hawaii where there is a lot of coral and sea grass.

On my last trip to the Aloha State, I changed to a pair of amber lenses with a more brownish tint and had a much easier time spotting these "ghosts of the flats." But when fishing the Southern California beaches in search of corbina cruising along shallow sandbars, I switched back to glasses I used in the Bahamas. The setting may be quite different, but the conditions for trying to spot fish are relatively similar. Light wave action, good water clarity, and midmorning sun can be ideal for picking out corbina sweeping the shallows in search of sand crabs, and the glasses you wear can make a huge difference in your ability to do so.

In contrast, when in deeper water like the offshore grounds where you're not going to see bottom, you generally do not have to be too concerned with singling out individual fish. When the occasion does arise and it's possible to actually see your quarry, the fish tend to be large and oftentimes very close to the surface, as is commonly the case with billfish species like striped marlin, sailfish, and swordfish. But even in these cases, the typical scenario is usually one where only a small part of the fish is visible, most often a portion of the tail or dorsal fin.

Fish like this corbina are not always so plainly visible when cruising the shore. This photo was taken at one of my favorite spots in Hermosa Beach, California. The corbina is a much sought-after game fish in Southern California that is easily accessible from the state's countless miles of open beachfronts.

Given the vastness of the ocean, trying to detect something this small is no easy task. Wavelets and all manner of floating debris can be deceiving. The fellows I knew who were the most accomplished at this were commercial sword fishermen who harpooned their fish. Even with spotter planes, this type of fishing normally entails logging countless hours up in the tuna tower scanning the surface with binoculars, trying to pick out a telltale fin. As sport fishers one way to mitigate the taxing demands of this visual game is to bring your quarry within casting distance by means of chum or establish preliminary contact by trolling teasers. But however one goes about pursuing fish in an offshore environment, generally optimum visibility will be achieved by wearing gray- or blue-tinted polarized glasses.

Wherever you fish and when light is a factor, make it a practice to wear a hat with a dark underbrim in conjunction with the glasses and you'll see even better. Since polarization does not provide optimum visibility at every angle, regardless of the color you choose, one useful trick when you're having difficulty discerning a particular object or form is to tilt your head slightly to one side. This helps alter the polarization and can provide a clearer picture of what you are looking at.

This is a shovelnose shark clearly visible only a few feet from the dry sand. They are not easy to entice with a fly.

This is the same shovelnose shown in the photo above. I followed it down the beach, made repeated casts, and finally succeeded in getting it to take a crab pattern.

Whether you're on the flats or fishing the deep blue open ocean, you want to train yourself to scan the water in a methodical pattern. The strategy is similar to that used by rescue operations on search missions. If you glue your eyes to one spot or randomly gaze at the surroundings in a haphazard fashion, you are likely to miss a lot. The fish themselves or various signs that may indicate their presence are likely to go unnoticed. To minimize this possibility, begin your search close to the boat or wherever you may be standing. Then at approximately 30-foot intervals start looking farther and farther out to just about the limit of your vision. Once you reach this point, start the process all over again.

If I were to summarize the topic of what to look for in a single sentence, it would be to simply look for anything that is out of the ordinary. This is where the services of an experienced guide can be considered your best fishing investment. If you are in shallow water and can clearly see the bottom, that is what you want to try to focus on. With the possible exception of barracuda (which often remain nearly motionless as they lie in wait to intercept their prey), most game fish are constantly swimming and any movement above the bottom can usually be easily detected. If there is only a couple of feet of water, you'll also have to be alert for surface signs like small wakes and fins protruding from the water. These provide some of the most exciting moments on the flats, and you have to learn to deliver the fly quickly and on target. Here speed and accuracy in your delivery are critical skills.

In deeper water most of your searching efforts will be directed at the surface. Aside from the fish themselves, perhaps the most telltale sign to be alert for are seabirds like frigates, terns, jaegers, seagulls, and pelicans. One of the laws of nature is that life-form follows life-form, and birds foraging and diving on the surface are typically sure signs that they are feeding on bait. And wherever you find concentrations of bait, there are inevitably schools of larger predator game fish ready to dine on them. If you are fortunate enough to experience it, you'll agree that the sight of large pods of baitfish being pursued by the birds above and the fish below is an event that can blow your emotional circuits.

Other signs may be less dramatic, but do not underestimate their importance. Any type of unusual surface disturbance can be a tip-off that fish may be in the area. For example, bait may reveal themselves by means of small wavelets or ripples on the surface. This is often referred to as "nervous water." Color changes can indicate temperature breaks, and fish like tuna are known to congregate near the edges where these changes occur. Any type of floating surface structure is worth looking at because in open expanses of water they often serve as havens for a variety of bait that attract larger predators. I've experienced some incredible offshore action on species like yellowtail and dorado that were congregating under kelp patties not much larger than a doormat.

In open water when you're casting to general areas you think might hold fish, the object is to cover as much water as possible, and long probing casts are generally the order of the day. For most open water and offshore applications, I generally opt for fast-sinking lines. Most of the action is down in the water column, but even under those circumstances where fish are breaking the surface, commencing the retrieve immediately after the fly hits the water at the conclusion of the forward cast will normally have your offering tracking through the fish's feeding zone.

Occasionally shore-bound anglers witness dramatic scenes like diving birds and breaking fish, but more often than not the signs of the surf tend to be far subtler. Reading the water in this environment is primarily based on learning to interpret wave action. The way waves behave as they roll into shore serves as an indication of what the bottom is like. Waves tend to break or crash over shallow areas, whereas they roll over deeper cuts or troughs in the bottom. Therefore, if you observe what looks like a relatively flat spot in the surf with waves crashing on either side, you are most likely looking at a patch of deeper water that is rolling over a depression in the

On the flats, once you've spotted your prey, you want to be as unobtrusive as possible in your approach. Crouching low as famed Oahu guide "ET" is doing here helps reduce your profile.

To be successful in the surf you have to learn how to read the beach. This photo shows an area of blue-colored water in the surf behind a wave break that indicates the presence of a bottom depression.

bottom. In most cases this is a prime spot to fish because a variety of small creatures ranging from crabs and worms to diminutive baitfish are swept into the calmer water of deep pockets, and larger predators establish feeding stations along the edges.

To the untrained eye, one stretch of water may look pretty much the same as any other. However, with a little practice you'll begin to see that this is not the case. You will also begin to experience a significant improvement in your hookup ratio versus the time you spend on the water.

4 Fly Lines for Salt Water

A shooting head (coiled) system is easy to work with and affords the angler on foot a great deal of versatility.

Aside from the size of the rod and reel combination you choose to fish, there are two additional decisions to make related to the presentation phase of the contest between you and the fish. The first has to do with what fly or pattern to select, which I take up later in the book. The second choice involves the type of fly line you decide to use to deliver the fly. Here choices have also multiplied, with a bewildering array of lines on the market.

The trick is to select a line that works best for the set of conditions you're dealing with. This can be especially challenging in a saltwater environment, where conditions in one locale can change within the hour just due to the effects of tide and current. Fishing success in these kinds of situations translates into the ability to adapt quickly, and fortunately today's fly lines make adjusting to changing conditions easier than ever. There is a fly line manufactured for practically every species and locale imaginable.

Floating Lines

There is no doubt that for freshwater fly-fishing applications, floating fly lines are the most popular choice, and in certain areas of the country like Florida and the Gulf states, they also tend to dominate the saltwater fishery. A full-length weight-forward floating fly line is what I learned to cast and fish with in the early '70s when I was living in the Northeast. Striped bass and bluefish were the primary targets, and because of their surface-feeding proclivities, there were many situations where floating lines were the most practical choice. In addition, the Northeast saltwater fly fishery was heavily influenced by South Florida practices that were (and still are) attuned primarily to shallow-water situations that saw little need for lines other than floaters.

My introduction to sinking lines had to wait a few years, when I moved back to the West Coast. Most West Coast saltwater fly fishing takes place in comparatively deeper water, so sinking lines predominate. In my present home waters about the only time a floating line is brought into play are those comparatively rare occasions where I can elicit surface strikes with a popper.

Having spent most of my fishing career on the West Coast, I became closely associated with sinking lines and shooting heads, but my favorite fly-fishing mode tends to be in the shallows (Louisiana redfish, bonefish in Hawaii, skinny-water stripers on the east end of Long Island, and snook and tarpon in South Florida) where I can use floating lines. But the fact remains that fly line choice should be a matter of adapting to prevailing conditions and not mere casting preference.

As is the case with sinking lines, once the decision is made to use a floater, there are still numerous styles to choose from, and this can be a source of confusion. A number of manufacturers label their lines focusing on a particular species; i.e., a bonefish line, a redfish line, a tarpon line, etc. This may be helpful if you are setting your sights on a particular species, but be mindful of the fact that these are not exclusive categories and there is considerable room for overlap. For example, you can effectively fish a line designated as a bonefish line for species as diverse as permit and redfish. Furthermore, if

Corbett Davis Jr. nailed this false albacore off Pensacola using a slow-sinking intermediate line. The albies were mopping up bait immediately below the surface, and this line carried the fly right where they were feeding.

you are fishing for bonefish, it doesn't mean you are out of the game because you don't have a line designated as a bonefish line.

For most shallow-water surface presentations, you cannot go wrong with a full-length, standard weight-forward floating line. One of my favorites in this category is a Royal Wulff line marketed as the 2-Tone Bermuda Triangle Taper. The line is designed for warmwater applications and has a color change to designate where there is sufficient line outside the rod tip to make an effective forward cast (this is sometimes referred to as the "sweet spot"). You can fashion a similar indication on a line that doesn't feature a color change by marking the line with a waterproof pen at the appropriate point. I recommend taking several casts before making the mark to be sure you have a spot that is comfortable for you.

The one problem with marking the line is that it may be difficult to see. At night this becomes practically impossible. To enable you to feel and possibly hear where this point has been reached, tie one or two six- to eight-turn nail knots on that section of line with a piece of 8- to 12-pound monofilament (we'll see how to tie these in the knot chapter).

The Bermuda Triangle Taper line has a 30-foot head section that I find makes for a smooth delivery with a variety of flies. There is a shorter head version (22- to 24-foot head) labeled as the Bermuda Triangle Short that is

Dorado like this one taken in Baja exemplify a species that depending on conditions can be taken using floating as well as sinking lines.

similar to RIO's Outbound Short. The shorter head sections on full-length floating fly lines are similar to the so-called bass bug tapers used by fresh-water fly fishers targeting largemouth bass with poppers. These blunt-head tapers are a better choice when casting wind-resistant poppers or when using a very fast-action rod. The downside is that they are not designed for delicate presentations and tend to strike the water hard. If you want to achieve the softest delivery possible when the fly turns over as the leader straightens, choose the weight-forward lines with the longer head sections.

Floating Line Casting Tips

One of the factors fly fishers like most about floating lines is that unlike their sinking counterparts that must be lifted up out of the water column, the line is already on the surface ready to be cast. No additional manipulation is necessary. However, to derive the maximum benefit of having the line resting on the surface, it's important to use proper technique at the very beginning stages of the cast.

For practice purposes, with a standard weight-forward floating line, lay about 30 feet of line out in front of you and try to take up as much slack as possible. Extend your rod hand out in front of you, and have the tip pointed right at the ground. The initial pickup method I'm about to describe is very similar to moving a garden hose across the lawn.

Pull and lift the rod in the same motion. The object here is getting the line to slide across the lawn or surface of the water prior to the actual liftoff. In contrast to simply ripping the line off the surface (doing so causes considerable noise and surface disturbance that will spook fish in the shallows), this gradual, upward glide path requires a nearly effortless casting stroke. More importantly, by starting slowly you can more effectively execute the all-important speed-up-and-stop motion critical to the formation of nice, tight loops. What happens is that in the process of creating a smooth upward and rearward flight path, the resistance of the line produces a gradual bend in the rod. This is what is commonly referred to as loading the rod. At a point when almost the entire line and leader have slid off the ground or water, accelerate your hand speed and then quickly make a definitive stop.

If you begin your casting stroke in this manner, in time you will notice that you will experience much less arm fatigue. Try it this way once, and then just try to abruptly pluck the line from the surface without pulling it toward you. You will quickly see that the latter technique requires a lot more effort. With practice you will also be amazed at how much line you can get airborne by simultaneously sliding it toward you and lifting upward.

Sinking Shooting Heads

Due in part to the dominant influence of South Florida on saltwater fly fishing, the subject of sinking lines, particularly in a shooting head configuration, has not been widely discussed in the fly-fishing literature. Some very narrow-minded provincial types didn't even consider the use of these to fall within the realm of fly fishing.

An extreme example of this disdain was displayed by a group of Northeast trout anglers who decided to fish at Casa Mar for a week. One fellow watched as I caught snook after snook in a bend in the river not far from the lodge. I could see he was using a floating line and not catching anything. I had my guide motor over to him, where we introduced ourselves and broached the topic of catching fish. He remarked how I was constantly into fish and asked what I was using. I showed him my setup and offered to rig a sinking shooting head for him, but he politely declined and informed me he "didn't fish that way." Lefty Kreh arrived in camp the next day and was able to convince some of these gentlemen that if they wanted to hook fish in these jungle rivers, they would have to get their flies down, and to do so they needed to

For bottom-hugging species like this halibut, a sinking shooting head is ideal for getting the fly down into their feeding zone.

Even when fish are on the surface, you are not necessarily at a disadvantage when using a sinking line. As was the case with this mako that was chummed to the surface, all you need do is begin retrieving the line as soon as the fly hits the surface, and in most cases the fly will still be in the fish's strike zone.

use fast-sinking lines. Practically any time I fish a sinking line, I opt for a shooting head system because I find it much easier to work with compared to a full-length sinking line.

The shooting head system consists of two separate lines: a relatively small-diameter running line and a larger-diameter shooting head normally joined to the running line via a loop-to-loop connection. The late casting champion Myron Gregory introduced me to this system back in the early 1970s. Myron was one of the first to use this setup in a casting tournament at the Golden Gate Casting Ponds in San Francisco in the 1930s. The combination of the thin-diameter running line being carried by the heavier head section is designed to afford maximum casting distance. When you have to make long-distance presentations or cover a lot of water, a shooting head system is an ideal choice.

For running lines (sometimes referred to as shooting lines), there are two basic choices: coated fly lines marketed as running lines and monofilament lines made specifically for this purpose. Just as with continuous-length lines, there is no perfect running line and each of the two have their devotees. One of the coated lines I can recommend is the Royal Wulff Tracer Shooting Line. It has a relatively small diameter (.032) that is ideal for most inshore fishing conditions.

Even though the water was shallow off this stretch of beach, a sinking line proved the appropriate choice for this corbina. Floating and intermediate lines will work in water this shallow, but in strong currents that frequently prevail in the surf, you'll find that sinking lines tend to track better in the turbulence.

Where mono running lines are concerned, opinion is greatly divided. Some swear by them, others swear at them. Unless thoroughly stretched, mono shooting lines are more prone to tangle than conventional running lines, and their lifespan is considerably shorter. Back in the '70s I used a mono line marketed as Cobra. It was flat and ultrasmooth as it ran across your finger. The problem was that it stretched like a piece of warm mozzarella cheese being pulled from a slice of pizza. For many years my old standby was Amnesia from the Sunset Line & Twine Company. Today the two monofilament running lines I most often fish are RIO's SlickShooter and the Varivas running line. Both are available in different tensile strengths with varying diameter. For big-game offshore applications I prefer a relatively large-diameter running line in the 50-pound class. For most inshore fishing I found the SlickShooter 40-pound-test line and Varivas's 36-pound-test line to work well.

What I like most about these mono running lines is that they are ultrasmooth shooting through the rod guides and it's very simple to fashion end loops in them. All you have to do is form a loop of the desired size and tie a double overhand (surgeon's) knot. To avoid having the tag end of the knot snag a rod guide, I take the extra step of mashing it down with pliers and whip-finishing it with fly-tying thread. Apply a protective coating to the threads with something like clear nail polish, and the loop-to-loop connection should be totally snag-free.

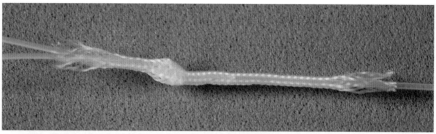
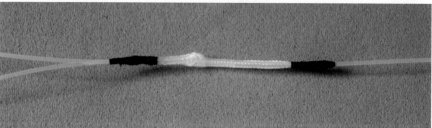

Top: Another method of smoothing over the connection is to slip a length of hollow-core braid over the surgeon's loop knot tied in the tag end of a monofilament running line.
Bottom: The braid is whip-finished at both ends with black fly-tying thread. The result is a mono running line loop that will pass snag-free through the rod guides.

All running lines are prone to tangles, but this is probably more often the case with mono lines. As a preventive measure, try to thoroughly stretch the line prior to use. Strip out the length of line you plan to cast, wrap it around a smooth stationary object, and pull on both sections, stretching it a bit as you do so. I used the trailer hitch on my van to do this. You can also stretch the line with just your hands. Wherever you happen to be standing—on a boat deck, the beach, etc.—pull out the length of running line you plan to cast and allow it to fall at your feet. Then begin stretching sections of the line with both hands, directing it into a basket or bucket.

This is a practice that will serve you well with all kinds of fly lines. The line will tend to lie more uniformly in the container, and the first fishing cast you make should go smoothly because the section of running line trailing directly behind the fly line head is the last section you stripped into the

I used 40-pound SlickShooter as my running line for the shooting head system I rigged on a San Diego albacore trip. Even though these fish will sometimes show on the surface chasing bait, the most consistent action is in the depths and that is where you want to present your fly.

container. Obviously this is the portion of line that is going to shoot up first, and it will do so unobstructed because it is lying on top. Conversely, if you tried making a cast without taking this step, a tangle will likely result because the sections of running line will be reversed; the forward section of running line will be at the bottom of the pile of line initially pulled from the reel's spool.

Traditionally the head portion of the shooting head system is 30 feet long. This makes changing lines very easy. All you do is coil the head around your hand, pass it through a 6- to 8-inch loop in the running line, secure it with something like a pipe cleaner, grab a different head, and interlock it with the running line loop. To do this with a standard full- length fly line that may run anywhere from 90 to over 100 feet in length would be a cumbersome process. This is one reason why shooting heads are ideal for the wading angler. It obviates the necessity of carrying an extra reel or spare spools. You can store several different type heads in a shirt or vest pocket and readily change lines with very little hassle.

Basing recommended line weights on full-length weight-forward lines, the standard practice is to up-line shooting head weights typically by two line sizes. Thus an appropriate shooting head for an 8-weight rod would be one with a 10-weight designation. For a 10-weight rod, you use a 12-weight shooting head. This can become confusing because there are some manufacturers who have up-lined their shooting heads and label them accordingly. For example, a line labeled as an 8-weight would be appropriate for an 8-weight rod. The best way to circumvent this problem is to select a shooting head by grain weight. I've found the following grain recommendations to be a useful guide: For an 8-weight fly rod, the head should weigh approximately 300 grains; a 9-weight rod will handle 350 grains; a 10-weight rod, 400 grains; an 11-weight, 450 grains; and a 12-weight, 500 grains.

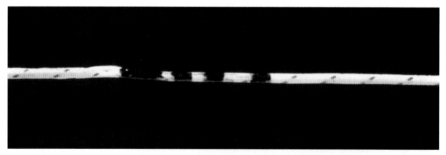

Marking a fly line with a waterproof pen makes it easy to determine its size. As a rule of thumb, a short dash designates the number 1, and a longer hash mark signifies the number 5. In the photo the line is an 8-weight (one 5 hash mark and 3 short dashes equal 8).

In terms of casting ease, for single-handed fly rods you generally would not want a head longer than 30 feet. With these rods you will find that heads over 30 feet begin to become more difficult to cast. This is simply due to the fact that the final forward cast should not be made until the entire length of the head and a portion of the running line (as a general rule of thumb, 3 to 6 feet of running line) are completely outside the rod tip. In casting parlance this short section of running line outside the tip-top is referred to as "over-hang." Often if I am making a custom head, I cut it to a length of about 27 or 28 feet. In practical fishing situations, particularly where you have limited room for a backcast, these shorter lines are easier to handle.

If you are just learning to cast, do not be misled by the mistaken claim that shooting heads are only for advanced casters. In fact, when teaching, the line I often put in the hands of first-time casters is a shooting head, usually one that is a floater. Because the weight of the line being cast is confined to this 30-foot section, even novice casters can readily begin to feel the line bend the rod on the back and forward strokes of the rod. To be a good caster you must be able to feel the line load (bend) the rod. In addition, the loop-to-loop connection gives a clear signal (you hear it and feel it as it passes through the rod guides) as to when the head is outside the tip-top, ready for the forward cast.

Despite these casting advantages, there are those who dislike the loop-to-loop configuration but nonetheless still want to use a shooting head–type line but one that is continuous, where the head blends seamlessly into the running line. These are referred to as integrated lines, and two examples I am familiar with and can recommend are the Royal Wulff Triangular Taper Saltwater Sinking Line and RIO's Striper26-foot Sink Tip line. One of the features I like about the Triangular Taper line is that the tip section can be cut to customize the line.

Sinking Head Casting Tips

The one advanced technique that should be mastered to effectively cast shooting heads (this applies to all fly lines) is the double haul that we'll treat shortly. A shooting head is designed to minimize false casts, and the double haul is the key to developing optimum line speed, eliminating the need for additional casting strokes.

To make an effective cast with a shooting head, the entire length of the head (e.g., 30 feet on a 30-foot head) must be completely outside the rod's tip-top. In addition, a section of the trailing running line must also extend past the tip-top. A common mistake made by those who are not familiar with these lines is to extend too much running line beyond the tip. When this happens you'll see the person wave the rod all over the place, with little or no movement imparted to the shooting head. This is because the small-diameter running line cannot support the thick, heavier shooting head. To get the head to move when you stroke the rod, you have to get it relatively close to the rod tip, and herein lies the one disadvantage of a shooting head system.

Even with a floating head, you are limited to the total length of line you are able to lift from the surface of the water. With a standard full-length floating line, an accomplished caster could lift upwards of 50 feet of line off the water—no time-consuming false cast is necessary. In contrast, this would not be possible with a shooting head. For this reason when fishing shallow water with floating lines, it is normally more practical to use a continuous full-length line instead of a shooting head. There is no precise standard, but as a working guideline anywhere from 2 to 5 feet of running line should be outside the rod tip. Every line and rod combination has its "sweet spot" in this respect, and with practice you will be able to quickly determine how much line you can effectively carry outside the rod tip.

When practicing your casts, it's OK to always begin with the entire head extended past the rod tip. But in fishing situations, especially with species like striped bass, which are notorious for tracking a fly a long distance before taking it practically at the angler's feet, it may be necessary to strip in line to the point where the shooting head is well inside the rod guides. When this is the case, to get it outside the rod tip in preparation for the next cast, you'll have to make a roll cast. If you are using a sinking shooting head, a roll cast will also be required to bring the head up out of the water column to the surface so you can take if off the water and make the cast (this is referred to as a water haul). Even if the head is only a few inches below the surface, as is often the case with a slow-sinking or intermediate line, before you can execute a cast the head must be brought to the surface, and the only way to get it there is by means of a roll cast. This is really the only reason novice casters find it easier to use floating lines—they're on the surface, ready to be cast.

Since you want to learn how to handle sinking lines, you'll want to practice on the water. Strip in the line to a point where the head and approximately 2 to 3 feet of running line are outside the rod tip. Next make a roll cast to bring the head to the surface. If you execute the roll cast properly, one roll cast is generally all it takes to accomplish this. However, if the head has sunk more than a few feet with a heavily weighted fly, you may have to make an additional roll cast to bring everything to the surface. With the line on the surface, immediately begin sliding it off the water for the backcast stroke. If you hesitate for a few seconds, the head will begin sinking and you'll have to begin again with another roll cast.

Execute the backcast with the easiest stroke possible. Go slow and smooth, both with the line haul (discussed below) and the speed-up-and-stop stroke with the rod. One of the most common mistakes made with these lines is going too fast and too hard. Instead, try to use just enough energy to throw the line behind you in a flat, straight path. Do the same on the forward cast stroke. The only difference is that on the forward cast you can make a sharper haul with the line hand. Also make a concerted effort to gradually accelerate the forward stroke, followed by a brief absolute stop with the rod hand. When you get it right, the line will rocket out over the water. With practice you'll also see that this is a very efficient way to cover the water because no time or effort is wasted making unnecessary false casts. Whenever I have to get a considerable depth below the surface and cover a lot of water, a shooting head system is my go-to setup.

Hauling for Distance

The shooting head is designed for distance, and that immediately raises the question, "Is distance all that important?" When instructing someone new to the game, I tell them not to worry about distance. When learning to cast you first have to focus on fundamentals; the distance factor comes later. In many, perhaps most, freshwater applications, how far you can present a fly usually is not critical to your fishing success. I have trout-fishing friends who rarely make a presentation more than 40 feet away. But it is a different story in the saltwater realm.

In fact, there are really only two scenarios in salt water where the need for long casts is generally not all that critical. One is shallow-water flats fishing. First off, many times you have to be fairly close just to be able to clearly see your quarry to make the proper presentation. In these conditions presentation is the name of the game, and day in, day out, it is speed and accuracy that pay more dividends than sheer distance. The other type of situation where casting distance often plays a secondary role is the big-game phase of the sport where species like billfish and sharks are being teased or chummed close to the boat.

That said, the hard reality is that distance is often the deciding factor when you're trying to get a fish to take your fly. As spin and conventional gear anglers well know, generally the more water you can cover, the greater the odds that a fish will intercept your offering. And then there are always

If you plan to fish salt water, you need to learn the double-haul casting technique to achieve optimum distance. Here I have just completed making the second haul as I stop the rod abruptly on the forward cast.

those maddening times when it is so difficult just to get the fly within range of fish you know are there. Anyone who has cast from a beach or a jetty wall knows this firsthand. The longest casts are often the only presentations that will result in a hookup.

This can be the case even when pursuing fish from a boat. A good case in point is trying to chase down members of the tuna clan like bonito, false albacore, bluefin, blackfin, and yellowfin. I've spent a great deal of time pursuing these ocean speedsters in the Northeast, the Florida Gulf, Mexico, Central America, and Southern California, and regardless of the locale, just trying to get within casting range can make you feel like you're chasing smoke. It seems every time you close to within 100 feet or so of a school, the fish would sound only to pop up again several hundred yards from where you're located. On many days if you didn't make casts of 80 feet or better, you didn't connect with any fish. There were so many times when my buddy Captain Scott Leon would call and vent his frustration because he had yellowfin tuna breaking 50 feet or so from the boat but his clients simply couldn't deliver the fly the required distance.

Making long casts is really all about achieving line speed. If you want to execute the former, you have to learn to generate the latter. As Lefty Kreh so clearly points out, the three factors necessary for achieving high line speed are a tight loop, a fast acceleration of the rod tip through the short distance where you make the speed-up-and-stop, and a very quick, abrupt stop.

Aside from executing the proper casting stroke, the second technique you need to master to generate more line speed is the double haul. A haul is simply a downward tug on the line during the cast. What it does is cause the rod tip to flex faster. To maximize its effectiveness, we make two hauls, one on the backcast and a second on the forward cast. The trick to combining the casting stroke with the tug on the line is to time the haul so that it occurs precisely at the moment you make the speed-up-and-stop motion. You will observe some casters yanking on the line like they were trying to pull-start a stubborn outboard motor, but this isn't necessary or efficient. Long pulls on the line will cause a deeper bend in the rod, which will enlarge the loop. It can also cause slack in the section of line that lies between your line hand and your rod hand. Ideally the distance you haul should be measured in inches, not in feet.

Aside from making hauls that are too exaggerated, the second most common fault in executing this technique is failing to have the line hand follow the rod hand during the backcast. The first haul on the backcast involves pulling your two hands apart. The line hand moves downward and slightly to the left (for right-handed casters). The moment it is completed, the line hand should immediately be raised and brought to within a foot or so of the rod hand, following it in its rearward movement. On the forward stroke the line hand remains in front of the rod hand and both the haul and the speed-up-and-stop are made simultaneously.

I have found that Lefty's method of teaching the double haul works best for most beginners. Instead of trying to execute hauls while continuously false casting, break the cast into two parts and do everything slowly. With about 25 feet of line outside the rod tip, slowly make a backcast and take a short, downward tug on the line at the moment you speed-up-and-stop. Allow the line to fall on the ground behind you. Think about what you just did. Were you able to do it correctly? If not, give it several more tries.

When you begin to get the feel of it, start making hauls on the forward cast, but keep both casts separate. Once you feel comfortable making the haul on the forward cast, you can begin to try making false casts with the double haul. If your timing is off, stop false casting and once again make a completely separate backcast with the haul, stop everything, and then make a forward cast with a haul. Work slowly and deliberately, and it will begin to come together.

You will also want to learn to vary the speed of the haul. The faster or sharper you tug on the line, the greater the line speed. Most people tend to haul at the same speed on both the backcast and forward cast. But since it is distance you are generally trying to achieve on the forward cast, haul sharper on the forward cast than you do on the backcast. However, if you are making a backcast presentation and need the distance, haul faster on the backcast. You will find that the double haul is such an efficient casting technique, you will use it every time you cast, even when distance is not a factor.

5 Two-Handed Rods in Salt Water

Executed properly, you can impart a deep bend in the rod. Here the rod is bent on the backcast. This will translate into a highly efficient forward cast that will deliver the fly out where it needs to be.

The use of double-handed rods in fly casting has a long, cherished tradition that dates back to the mid-1800s when they were being used on the River Spey in Scotland. The Spey cast is defined as a dynamic roll cast that allows the angler to change the direction of the cast. In its classic form, primarily anglers in pursuit of Atlantic salmon used it and it was a pastime basically limited to the well-heeled. Common folk had neither the time, the means, nor the access to fish the prime river "beats."

Though sturdy wooden skiffs were used, the common practice was to wade and basically roll cast a long-belly fly line across a wide expanse of river. This type of fishing was all about controlling the fly as it swung in the current. There was little or no manual manipulation of the fly. At the conclusion of the swing downcurrent, instead of stripping the fly in for a given distance, different forms of roll casts were developed whereby the angler repositioned the fly in preparation for the next delivery out into the current.

With the benefit of modern science, today's Spey rods and lines are quantum leaps ahead of their predecessors. However, the prospect of effectively casting long-belly lines where roughly 60 to 70 feet or more of line must be outside the rod tip is no easy task, and it requires a great deal of practice to get it right.

I first saw them in action when I was living in San Francisco close to the famed Golden Gate Casting Ponds. Some of the world's great casters gather here, and I became fascinated with these casts when I observed practice sessions with luminaries who were preparing for the Golden Gate Angling & Casting Club's annual Spey-O-Rama. The casts are visually compelling, and the sensation of going through the motions is far different from what

This is one of the the famed Golden Gate Casting Ponds in San Francisco—a great place to hone your casting skills with two-handed rods.

you experience with an overhand cast using a single-handed rod. I became enamored with it and was not about to miss out on an opportunity to learn from some of the sport's masters. However, despite the pure exhilaration of this casting style, for fishing purposes here in the United States, there is not a great deal of application for these extreme long-belly lines in either fresh or salt water.

Overseas, when Spey casting spread farther north, the Scandinavians developed modifications more suitable to their fishery and began using what are essentially shooting head–style lines that are considerably shorter than the long-belly Spey lines. For several decades a select segment of anglers in our Pacific Northwest began using two-handed rods and the shorter Spey lines primarily for their steelhead fishery. In the last few years there has been a significant upswing in their popularity among US-based fly fishers, and a growing number are beginning to fish them in the salt.

Back in 2000 when I made an eight-year sojourn back to the waters of my youth in the Northeast, I was one of the few to use two-handed rods off the beach. Initially I wasn't making Spey-type casts; instead I was using the double-handed rod to cast overhead. I wanted increased distance, and the

One of the attributes of a two-handed rod is that it can give added distance with minimal effort. This is making it an increasingly popular choice for use in the surf.

11- to 14-foot rods I began using enabled me to reach fish (primarily bluefish and stripers) that normally would have been out of range for a single-handed 9-foot fly rod. It's a matter of simple physics. The rod functions as a lever, and the longer the lever, the easier it is to accomplish the task. With the two-handed rods I was able to hit and exceed the "magic" 100-foot mark even with the ever-present onshore wind.

Obviously, because they are longer than their single-handed counterparts, double-handed rods are going to be quite a bit heavier. You will also need large-capacity reels to accommodate the larger-diameter lines normally used with two-handed rods. But this is offset by the fact that you are using both hands, and when properly executed this casting method can actually be less tiring than fishing with a single-hand rod.

A second major advantage is the nature of the backcast loop that is formed with a Spey cast. Unlike the backcast loop formed with an overhead cast, the backstroke in a Spey cast forms a loop (referred to as a D-loop) that develops underneath the rod tip. It never fully extends behind you, and a portion of the line touches down on the water (this is referred to as an anchor). Because the line never fully extends behind, less room is needed for the backcast. With the shorter Spey lines like the Skagit, for example, you can form a D-loop even when the space behind you is limited. This means you can fish in a lot of places where it would be almost impossible to make a traditional overhead backcast. Potential casting obstacles like trees, brush, and rocks can be easily avoided.

Longer two-handed rods also give you more line control. This can be a major concern for anglers like steelhead buffs who fish fast-moving water like the flows typically encountered in strong river currents. But saltwater anglers presenting their flies in strong tidal flows will also find the longer double-handed rod to be more effective for mending the line and controlling the fly on the swing. Line control, or more specifically line placement of the fly, is also made a tad safer because the fly can be positioned in front of you at a safer angle for the cast.

Last but certainly not least is the fact that casting two-handed rods is a great deal of fun. One of my steelhead buddies summed it up nicely when he said, "If steelhead are a fish of a thousand casts, you may as well have a good time making all those casts." If you have never fly cast before, there is nothing wrong beginning your new sport with double-hand rods. For seasoned fly fishers, picking up a two-handed rod and learning to use it properly will dramatically increase your window of fishing opportunities.

Due to their added length, two-handed rods generally make for more efficient casting instruments compared to shorter one-handed sticks. However, when it comes to fighting fish, that added length can put double-handed rods at a disadvantage simply because the fish at the other of the line now has the longer part of the lever working in its favor. The effect is like a seesaw when one person sits on a lengthier portion of the board. Even if that person weighs less, the increase in the board length on their side of the pivot point can be enough to offset the weight differential, so the lighter person on the longer portion of the board will cause the board to dip to the ground. For this reason alone, I wouldn't choose a double-handed rod for fishing species like tuna that characteristically plummet to the depths after being hooked. You would be at a tremendous disadvantage trying to pump a fish like this up from the depths.

Additionally, due to their added length, two-handed rods tend to be unwieldy in the confines of a boat, and the casting distance they afford isn't as critical a factor as it is for the shore-bound angler. It's in wade-fishing applications when you're making repeated casts trying to cover as much water as possible where double-handed rods come into their own. In terms of fish-fighting effectiveness, because wading water depths seldom approach that which you could encounter from a boat, the rod's longer length seldom poses any significant handicap in fighting fish.

As in all fly casting, using the correct fly line is critical, and where two-handed rods are concerned, the important consideration is the fact that these longer rods will require a much heavier grain weight compared to a similarly rated single-handed rod. For example, a 9-foot 8-weight single-handed rod might cast very well with a 300-grain line. But step up to something like a 12½-foot stick with the same 8-weight designation, and you'll likely find that it will require a line in the range of 500 to 600 grains.

Similar to the case with single-hand rods, the head length of the fly line for overhead and Spey-type casts with two-handed rods is an important consideration. As stated in the previous chapter on shooting heads, in actual fishing situations shorter head lines (i.e., 27 to 30 feet) are more user-friendly than longer belly lines. In addition, longer belly lines are not a particularly good choice in sinking line applications or when using heavily weighted flies because it is more difficult to bring all this to the surface to make a cast.

The Overhead Cast

For most novices the easiest cast to master with a double-hand rod and one that is perhaps used most in saltwater applications is the overhead cast.

The basic difference between using a single-hand rod and a double-hand rod for an overhead cast is the method by which the cast is physically

Overhead casting on a foggy morning at Torrey Pines State Beach, California, with one of my favorite two-handed rods for the Southern California surf, a 5-weight TFO BVK.

executed. This may seem obvious, but regardless of the type of cast being executed, the major problem most people face when picking up a two-handed rod is actually using both hands to make the cast.

First off, you want to adopt a proper grip. Since we are using a double-handed rod, this obviously involves placement of both hands. There are variations in the exact details of positioning, but from a right-handed caster's perspective, basically you want to place your left hand on the rod butt and your right hand in the middle area or top portion of the upper grip above the reel. It is especially important with the right-hand placement to cradle the rod firmly but not too tightly. If you have something approaching a death grip on the upper portion of the handle, there will be a tendency to overpower the rod (push too hard) on the forward cast—something you definitely want to avoid.

Because these rods feel big and heavy compared to single-handed sticks, the natural inclination is to try to muscle them during the cast, especially with the rod hand. Instead, you want to go as easy as possible with this hand. The main function of the right hand (or the left hand for left-handed casters) is to simply cradle the rod and guide it through the casting strokes. The real work is going to be accomplished by the hand on the rod butt. In this sense you can think of the left hand as performing the function of the double haul. But instead of pulling on the line with this hand as you do with a single-handed rod, the left hand generates line speed as you push the rod butt away from you on the backcast and pull it back toward you during the forward cast.

"Assume the position" is the appropriate phrase for the second step in the process. For a right-handed caster this means placing your left foot in front of you. It shouldn't be as exaggerated as a dance step, but there will be a moderate rocking motion as you lean back on the right foot with the backcast and then shift weight to the left foot during the forward cast. Even though you may not do so when casting with a single-handed rod, because this is a new technique, I recommend looking over your right shoulder to monitor your backcast. Before you begin to develop a feel for these rods you have to know what's going on with your backcast, and the best way is to turn your head and see for yourself. As is true for the single-handed rod, a proper backcast is a necessary prerequisite for making an effective forward cast.

With two-handed rods you will find that it only takes a slight hand motion to move the rod tip a considerable distance. But to achieve tight loops, which translate into added distance, you want a very abbreviated speed-up-and-stop motion in your casting strokes. This is necessary when using conventional single-handed rods and even more critical where long, two-handed rods are involved. Any exaggerated hand movement is multiplied with the longer rod. For example, the same hand movement will cause the rod tip to travel considerably farther on a 14-foot rod than it will on a 9-foot rod, and too much tip travel will result in big, wide loops. A physicist will tell you that a wide loop is the result of energy that has been scattered over a wide arc that dissipates the force you're trying to generate. In simple terms, the fat loop isn't going to travel very far.

For the right-handed caster, begin the backcast by tucking your right elbow fairly close alongside your body just above the waist. Point the rod tip low to the water. In one smooth motion, raise your right arm. At the same time push the butt section of the rod out away from you with the left hand. Similar to a single-hand backcast, allow the rolling loop of line to nearly completely straighten out behind you. The cast will be compromised if you wait until the line is completely straight behind you. What you want is a sort of candy cane loop in the line unfolding behind you just before you begin making the forward stroke. That is why it's a good idea for novice casters to glance backward and see what's happening. Executed correctly in conjunction with the outward push of the rod butt, the rod will flex practically its entire length. Avoid the tendency to push out hard with the right hand on the forward cast. If you do so the result is a rod flex that is confined primarily to the tip

It's important to stop the rod high on the conclusion of the forward cast with a double-handed rod. The slightest dip downward will be exaggerated due to the rod's length. This will open the loop, robbing you of distance.

section. This will rob you of considerable distance because you are only using a portion of the rod to propel the line.

The forward cast is executed by simultaneously lowering the right elbow back down to your body while pulling the rod butt in tight to your waist. This will create a nice, high stop on the forward cast. When you do it right, you will feel the full flex of the rod and the line will rocket out past the tip. If you find yourself experiencing problems with the forward cast, it will most likely be due to two common faults typically exhibited by novice double-handed casters: overpowering the forward stroke with the rod hand, and failure to stop the rod tip high. To help correct this, bear in mind that you are using a long lever. Compared to a shorter, single-handed rod, you also have more line delivering power at your disposal. You don't want to compromise this by providing a great deal of extra input with your rod hand. In addition, the long-lever effect of a double-handed rod means that even a slight over-stroke on the forward cast is likely to be more pronounced than would be the case with a single-handed rod. In both instances over-stroking diminishes the rod's flexing characteristics, resulting in a big fat loop and reduced line speed.

The Skagit Cast

Probably the second most popular casting style used by anglers fishing two-handed rods in the salt is the Skagit cast. It takes its name from the Skagit River in Washington, where it originated. It's a type of Spey cast that uses a waterborne anchor. In this respect it bears similarity to the water haul used for casting sinking lines overhead with both single- and doubled-handed rods. Before you can make the forward cast, the line that has sunk beneath the surface must be brought back to the surface. This is accomplished by means of a simple roll cast. With the line on the surface you make a backcast by sliding the line off the water. Remember it is the resistance of the line in the water that bends (loads) the rod.

With a single-hand rod, you make one backcast followed by the forward cast. However, the technique differs somewhat when using a Skagit line. These are short-belly (they can range from approximately 20 to 27 feet long) large-diameter heads, most of which float. They all require tip sections (loop-to-loop connections make for quick and easy line changes) that are available

The Skagit setup is ideal for wade fishing bays and estuaries. This is a choice spot on the southern section of San Diego Bay.

in different floating/sinking configurations that afford a great deal of versatility for all kinds of fishing conditions. The tips can vary in length anywhere from 5 to 15 feet.

Because the bellies are shorter, thicker, and heavier than traditional Spey lines, Skagit casting is somewhat easy for novice casters to learn. The short and relatively heavy lines make it possible to execute relatively long casts in situations where there is little room behind you. They are also designed to lift deeply sunken tips and large, heavy flies. In an effort to maintain a constant ratio between rod length and the line's head length, as a rule the belly length may be three or even four times the rod length.

As is the case with other shooting head systems, to make the cast begin by stripping the head in toward the rod tip, leaving approximately 2 to 3 feet of running line outside the tip-top. You want the fly positioned at roughly a 45-degree angle to the side you are casting from. There are a number of ways to reposition the fly (a snap T move, for example), but the easiest move is by means of what is referred to as a Perry Poke.

Try to make this entire sequence—from dropping the rod tip to the conclusion of the sweep and the snap forward—in one continuous, smooth motion. An expression I like to use when teaching this cast to beginners is to "believe in the rod." It's a shorthand way of saying that in all casting forms you have to learn to use the full capacity of the rod's function as the principal lever. Lefty Kreh is fond of saying, "Cast smarter, not harder."

Perry Poke Sequence

Left: The Perry Poke consists of two steps. Bring the rod toward you to where it rests up against the shoulder of your casting arm. The Skagit body should be lying slightly to your right side (on your left if you're casting with that hand). For right-handed casters, do this by simultaneously pushing the rod butt out with your left hand and lifting the rod slightly toward your shoulder with the rod hand.

Below: Lower the rod tip to the opposite side of your rod hand. In this photo it's to the left. This should cause the Skagit head to form a rough semicircle on the surface in preparation for the sweep. For a right-handed caster, the sweep will be directed to the right. If there is a strong current, you may have to make several Perry Pokes to get the fly positioned in front of you and out to the right.

Above: The next step is appropriately referred to as the sweep. Keep the rod tip close to the water and sweep the rod to your right. Make the sweep by pushing the rod butt out with the bottom hand. It helps to act as if you were vacuuming the line off the water. As you near the end of the sweep, the Skagit body should be swept off the water with approximately half the length of the tip section remaining in the water.

Below: The sweep has been completed. Your left or bottom hand should be positioned out in front of you. This positioning is important because snapping the rod butt into your chest area is how you make the forward cast. At the conclusion of the sweep, the rod is raised with the tip pointed fairly high toward the horizon. The rod butt is snapped sharply into the chest with the bottom hand while the rod is pushed forward, followed by an abrupt stop. The rod hand does very little. Its primary function is to cradle the rod and serve as a fulcrum point. Remember that the rod functions as a relatively long lever, so if you punch it forward, it will open the loop and ruin the cast. Instead, use the rod hand to help bring the rod to a short, abrupt stop with the tip pointing high.

Above: The very beginning of the forward cast. Note that for a right-handed caster, the left hand on the rod butt is positioned out away from one's body. The rod hand abruptly stops the rod movement rearward.

Below: Execute the forward cast by sharply snapping the rod butt in toward your chest while simultaneously gently pushing the rod forward and immediately stopping its movement.

Above: The conclusion of the forward cast, side view. Note that the rod tip is pointed high at the end of the stroke.

Below: Rear view of the conclusion of the forward cast.

Fishing Skagit Style

It wasn't long after I began fishing two-handed rods, making overhead casts off beachfronts in the Northeast, that I decided to try using these rods making Skagit-style casts. Truthfully the transition wasn't all that easy because there was no one available to give me hands-on instruction. I read a lot on the subject and studied some videos that helped get me started, but in all undertakings of this nature, your best course is to seek out personal instruction from someone who has mastered these casts and is able to convey their skills to others. I consider myself fortunate in that I didn't develop major faults that would take a lot of work to correct later on.

My knowledge and years of experience with single-handed rods—particularly with shooting heads, much of which applies to Skagit casting—were certainly helpful, as well as the fact that I had direct access to Long Island Sound from my waterfront condo in Westbrook, Connecticut. You really need water to make these casts, and weather conditions permitting, I practiced on a daily basis. At first I stood on the condominium dock bordering a tidal river that ran into the sound. The setting was ideal because there was little room for a backcast and depending on the tidal stage, current would run either to my right or my left, forcing me to practice with my right and left top hands to accommodate either direction.

Using a two-handed rod on a scenic beachfront in San Francisco.

Quite unexpectedly it was on the dock where I encountered my first Skagit striper. For safety purposes I wasn't using a fly tied on a hook. Instead, I simulated the size and weight of the different flies I planned to use by tying various concoctions on different-size cotter pins. Sometime around the second week of a late-spring practice session, I felt a strong grab on the yarn "fly" that was swinging in the current. Simultaneously I could see the fish flash as it intercepted what it probably mistook for a small herring. All thoughts of practice quickly left me. I reeled in the line, left the outfit on the dock, ran back up to the condo, and grabbed half a dozen flies. Probably not more than 20 minutes later, I was into my first Skagit striper.

Even though my technique would require considerable more polish, from then on my "practice" sessions were transformed into fishing sessions. The river was only about 70 feet wide, and it became easy to launch casts to the other side of the bank. The bank was undercut and provided a convenient ambush station for stripers lurking for baitfish swept in by the current. Over the next few weeks I took several more stripers, but the condo dock wasn't the most productive spot and I was looking forward to early June when I could start fishing the mouth of the harbor and a couple of nearby islands. In addition to my standard single-hand outfit, I began taking a two-handed rod out on my kick boat. On numerous occasions I fished the two-handed rod from the kick boat, casting it both overhead and Skagit style.

Admittedly fishing a double-handed rod from a craft like this is more a matter of personal preference where the issue of practicality is only a secondary consideration. The point I made at the beginning of this chapter about two-handed rods being a less-than-ideal choice when fishing from boats is even more applicable in the case of personal watercraft like kick boats. You are sitting inches off the water, and the casting motion is limited entirely to your upper body. Nonetheless it is certainly doable and I enjoyed every minute I used the long rod in this fashion, casting it both overhead and Skagit style. In addition, casting from a seated position where you can't bring your hips and legs into play forces you to hone the casting stroke to the point where you're making the rod do most of the work, and this will pay dividends on those occasions when you cast from a standing position.

Given the added length of double-handed rods and the restricted movement in a craft like a kayak or kick boat, the major challenge I faced was bringing a spent fish to within reach so I could remove the fly and release my catch. The technique I used is described at the end of the chapter in the discussion of releasing fish when wading.

Despite the fun I had fishing two-handed rods from the kick boat, my primary objective was to Skagit cast with these rods when I used the craft primarily to transport me to places where I wanted to get out and wade fish.

The author with a two-handed rod blind casting to bonefish in Hawaii.

Hooked up on an Oahu bone with the long rod.

The mouth of the harbor was one such spot, and the most efficient way to fish it was on foot. In this respect it was like a classic steelhead river. Proceeding from the harbor mouth, I rowed to the left side opposite the jetty, pulled the kick boat up on a sandbar, and waded out to fish the steep sloping edge. I fished this area many times with single-handed rods, so I had a good frame of reference to evaluate the effectiveness of standard 9-foot rods versus their longer double-handed counterparts.

I didn't document my catch rate, but it's safe to say that there wasn't much difference in the number of bass I caught with a single-hand rod versus a Skagit setup. It's really more a matter of which style you prefer. However, aside from subjective preferences, the longer double-handed rod did make it easier to mend line as it swung in the current. Even though they were heavier, I also found Skagit casting with the double-handed rods considerably less tiring when I fished all day through both tidal cycles. If you think about it, you are not slinging a relatively long line in the air as is the case with overhead casts. The Skagit is a waterborne cast, there is minimal arm movement, and you're using both hands.

Aloha Bones

Some of my most memorable Skagit fishing experiences are with bonefish in Hawaii. A few of the locals on Oahu have been using two-handed rods for blind casting to bonefish in waist-deep water. To some diehard flats anglers, mere mention of blind casting to bonefish will elicit a very negative reaction. They will steadfastly maintain that the only proper way to go about this with fly gear is to do it visually. My response is that this is a purely subjective consideration.

Even among local fly fishers on Oahu, opinion is divided on what bonefishing method is more fun. Blind casting itself does not violate any IGFA standard, and it's rather fruitless to argue the merits of either case. Personally, I enjoy using both approaches. Admittedly, before I ever tried using two-handed rods in this manner, I was a little skeptical. I had taken many stripers with a Skagit setup, but bonefish never seemed to be a viable target. However, after my first trip when I saw some of the locals doing it, I definitely wanted to give it a try.

One of the fellows who pioneered using a two-handed rod for Hawaiian bonefish is Clayton Yee. He was born and raised in Hawaii but attended college in Oregon, where he caught the steelhead bug. He became very proficient with double-handed casting and soon started adopting it for his home waters.

My first experience with blind casting on the island (they refer to it as "bombing") was with a good friend of Clayton's, Doug Lum. Doug is one of the masters of the visual game, but this particular day turned overcast and even his well-practiced eyes were not picking out fish. Hawaii is a long trip even from California; he knew I was anxious to pull on some fish and asked if I wanted to wade a little deeper and try bombing a few casts. At the time I was fishing a standard 9-foot 8-weight fly rod that I brought along for sight-fishing. Luckily this option turned out to be very successful, and even though I couldn't see the take, the sensation of the strike and resulting struggle were classic bonefish and I had a good time.

For my next trip over, I brought along a 12½-foot 6-weight Pandion rod I helped design for Temple Fork Outfitters (TFO). I matched it with a 525-grain Skagit line and 8-foot intermediate tip. There was no question that for making repeated casts for hours on end, this setup proved a lot easier physically than double-hauling and overhead casting with a single-handed rod.

Due to the legendary wariness of bonefish and the relatively shallow water, clear intermediate sink tips are used. Their comparatively slow sink rate will also help prevent the fly from getting fouled on the ever-present chunks of coral that inundate the bottom. However, rocks and coral can take their toll on leaders, so in most of the places on the island, many of the locals recommend 20-pound test for the class tippet. Given the fact that these fish often

Appropriately so, bonefish are often referred to as the "ghosts of the flats."

exceed the 5-pound mark, you won't feel over-gunned with tippets this size. In cases where the fish manages to get into shallow water, pointing the long rod overhead can help clear a multiplicity of hazards like coral, lava, and mangrove shoots.

What about the prospect of using a Skagit setup for shallow-water sight-fishing? I managed to do it with a tailing bone in Hawaii, but it's not a practical option. The disadvantage in doing so has more to do with the nature of this cast, not the length of the rod itself. As discussed above, the Skagit cast uses the resistance created by drawing the large-diameter Skagit body across the surface to help load the rod for the forward cast. But sweeping the line across the water creates surface disturbance as well as noise, and this can pose a serious obstacle in fishing situations where stealth is a primary consideration. On shallow-water flats this kind of disturbance is sure to spook fish. Normally any time fish enter shallow water, even if they are there to feed, they become especially wary and the noise and disturbance generated by these types of casts can easily put them off.

The one successful hookup I experienced was with a tailing bonefish that was about 80 feet in front of me. I had just waded in from deeper water to see how Doug was doing in the shallows. He pointed out the tailing bone and told me to try making a cast to it. Due to the distance, the fish apparently was not disturbed as I swept the line across the surface. The fly landed approximately 15 feet to the left of the bone, who was still preoccupied with rooting out food items on the bottom. As it started to swim in the direction of my fly, I made a couple of slow, short strips and it took. The large-arbor reel I was using quickly emptied and Doug in his typical understated manner said, "This is a good fish." Unfortunately we never were able to get a close-up view. There were mangroves in the direction it was running, and because so much line was out in the water, even lifting the long rod overhead did not have the desired effect. We parted company.

Though bonefish are the primary target, when you blind cast you never know what you might connect with, and in these waters there's always a chance of hooking into members of the jack family like the incredibly strong pulling trevally. They all pull hard and can make line smoke off your reel at an alarming rate.

Heading Back to the Mainland

About 3,000 miles east of the islands, I'm also Skagit casting in my home waters along the California coastline. When I lived in San Francisco the target species was striped bass, and similar to the conditions I fished in the beach locales of Long Island Sound, one of my favorite spots was a picturesque stretch of shore known as Crissy Field.

Burt Rances, to whom I owe much for the time he spent helping me become proficient with two-handed rods, practicing his craft off the beach in San Francisco Bay.

For years I taught classes in criminal justice, and one of my specialties was prison systems. I never dreamed that one day I would be fishing a spot that was directly across from Alcatraz Island. Because you are fishing inside San Francisco Bay (the Golden Gate Bridge will be on your left), there is not much in the way of surf to contend with, but the current can be very strong. I've had 600-grain lines sweep past me like leaves being blown across a field by a strong wind. This also confirmed my belief that it isn't likely that anyone ever managed to swim off the island and reach the mainland.

Nonetheless, it's the kind of shorefront that's an ideal spot for Skagit casting. The area is free from structure, but in making conventional overhead backcasts, you have to constantly monitor what's going on behind you in the form of casual beach strollers, joggers, and packs of city dogs overjoyed by the opportunity to frolic along the shore. Wading only a few feet into the water executing Skagit casts will generally ensure that you'll be clear of these potential obstacles.

Off Southern California the primary species I target with a Skagit system are surfperch, halibut, and yellowfin croaker. But regardless of the beachfront, the same advantages I found using this setup in other locales also applies to Northern and Southern California shorelines. Physically the Skagit setup can be a lot easier on you when you have to make repeated casts. Even when sweeping the line across the surface in preparation for the forward cast, executed correctly the motion is smooth and easy, and coupled with a minimalist forward cast motion, it's possible to achieve good distance with comparatively little effort.

Secondly, as stated above, another big plus is the fact that even in those places where there's adequate room for overhead backcasts, the Skagit cast doesn't require much space behind you, so it's ideal any time your casting lanes are restricted. Particularly in some of the harbors I waded in the Northeast in search of stripers, when overhead casting with a single-handed rod, occasionally I found myself snagging a mooring line on one of the boats crowding the area. When I switched to a Skagit setup, this seldom became an issue.

Thirdly, though not confined to Skagit lines, the different tip sections that are available make for incredible versatility. Tip additions have been available for single-hand weight-forward fly lines for quite some time, but most do not cast as well as an uninterrupted length of a standard weight-forward line. In contrast, because they are an integral part of the Skagit system, tip sections blend seamlessly with the line's heavy body, and the line lies out smoothly at the conclusion of the cast. In the section on shooting heads, I stated that one of the virtues of the head system is the fact that one head can be easily changed for another. It's even easier with Skagit tip sections. Most are only a third of the length of a shooting head, so it's really easy to change one tip section for another. Just make sure there's an end loop in the leader so it can be quickly interconnected with the tip's end loop. Having the ability to

Burt Rances and Al Tom working the water in San Francisco Bay with Alcatraz in the background.

quickly make adjustments for different depths and changing tidal currents can be a real asset.

For example, even though most Southern California beachfronts have a gradual shallow slope seaward, there are troughs and tidal currents that affect a fish's feeding behavior, and the depth at which the fly is riding in the water column is an important determining factor as to whether a fish will commit to taking your fly. For years with single-handed rods I always tried to adhere to a policy of applying as little weight as possible to get the fly to the appropriate depth. It's no secret that a lighter fly is easier to cast than its more heavily weighted counterpart, so whenever possible I try to rely on the line to deliver the fly to the proper depth.

To get a fly deeper in the water column, the common practice is to simply change to a more heavily weighted fly. When fishing from a boat, where I carry a large number of flies in different weight configurations, this is something I normally would do. But often when wade fishing, I carry a minimal number of flies, and for the shorelines I am most familiar with, I know that certain patterns work very well because I have years of success fishing them. Many of these patterns are tied with small dumbbell eyes, and I do not want to weight them any heavier. In very shallow areas I can fish them with slow-sinking or intermediate lines, but if I find a spot on the beach where there's a well-defined trough and I need to get the fly deeper in the water column, I'll switch to a fast-sinking tip. Fishing beachfronts like Northern California and the Northeast where features such as boulders and rock out-croppings, steep drop-offs, and fierce tidal currents can often be found within a short walk of each other, the ability to readily change tip sections to adjust the fly's depth can be a real game-changer.

The two-handed rods I prefer for this generally range in length from 11½ to 13½ feet or so. More so than the particular species I may be fishing, the size of the flies I'm casting are the main determining factor in what weight rod I choose. For my particular situations where the fish are comparatively small by saltwater standards, I opt for TFO's 4-weight switch rod (I primarily overhead cast with this rod) and occasionally the Pandion 6-weight. The switch rod, as its name implies, is designed to be cast either single- or doubled-handed. But due to their added length (most are 11 to 12 feet), I find it tiring to make more than a few single-hand casts with these rods. I always use them for double-handed casts. In beach-fishing locales like the Northeast where stripers and bluefish are my primary targets, I generally opt for the Pandion 8-weight to handle larger streamer patterns.

One problem you may face Skagit casting in the surf is the backwash. Particularly when the surf is running strong, the water rushes back off the beach and that can cause you to lose your anchor point. At times like these

I forgo Skagit casts and start slinging the line overhead. My objective in helping design the Pandion series was to have a rod fully capable of casting a Skagit line both Skagit style and overhead. The Pandion series offers great versatility in this respect.

Nick Conklin with TFO has become enamored with double-handed rods, and through countess hours of casting and testing, he came up with the recommended Skagit and overhead casting line chart on page 83 for our Pandion rod series.

Some months after Nick put this chart together, we both discovered a new series of Skagit lines while working at the 2016 Spey-O-Rama championships at the Golden Gate Casting Ponds in San Francisco. These innovative lines are marketed under the label of Olympic Peninsula Skagit Tactics and are referred to as Commando Heads. They are the product of two Skagit pioneers, Ed Ward and Jerry French. What sets these lines apart is their comparatively short length (depending on grain weight, they range from 12 to 18 feet), which makes them ideally suited to what is referred to as a Sustained Anchor Systemology.

As in all Skagit tactics, the cast utilizes a waterborne anchor. But given their abbreviated length, the cast is made in one continuous motion; there is no momentary pause just before the final forward stroke. Because the

Burt Rances with his typically well executed back cast.

Pandion Line Recommendations

	Skagit	Two-Handed Overhead	Mid-belly	Long-belly	Other
6-weight 12'9" 4-piece	380–480 grains 20- to 26-foot heads RIO Skagit Max RIO Skagit iFlight Airflo Skagit Compact Airflo Rage Compact	380–450 grains 18- to 22-foot heads RIO Skagit Max Short RIO Skagit iFlight RIO Skagit iShort Scientific Anglers Skagit Extreme	400–420 grains 40–48.5 feet Scientific Anglers Spey Evolution RIO Short Head Spey	*	RIO Switch Chucker (#7, 465 grains)
8-weight 13'3" 4-piece	500–570 grains 22- to 28-foot heads RIO Skagit Max RIO Skagit iFlight Airflo Skagit Compact Airflo Rage Compact	480–550 grains 22- to 26-foot heads RIO Skagit Max Short RIO Skagit iFlight RIO Skagit iShort Scientific Anglers Skagit Extreme	500–540 grains 40–48.5 feet Scientific Anglers Spey Evolution RIO Short Head Spey	*	RIO Switch Chucker (#9, 570 grains)
9-weight 13'9" 4-piece	600–725 grains 23- to 30-foot heads RIO Skagit Max RIO Skagit Max Long RIO Skagit iFlight Airflo Skagit Compact Airflo Rage Compact	580–640 grains 20- to 26-foot heads RIO Skagit Max Short RIO Skagit iFlight RIO Skagit iShort Scientific Anglers Skagit Extreme	550–650 grains 40–53 feet Scientific Anglers Spey Evolution RIO Short Head Spey	*	*

rod is loaded from the resistance of the waterborne anchor, the smooth continuous stroke makes for a very efficient delivery, something that can be easily executed even with shorter 9-foot single-handed rods. Because this system is new (at least at the time of this writing), I haven't had a chance to accumulate a great deal of fishing time with it, but I'm very impressed with the heads I've cast thus far and can definitely recommend them for those interested in Skagit casting.

Retieving, Striking, and Playing Fish on Double-Handed Rods

Similar to when I'm fishing single-handed rods, with the two-handers I use both the conventional single-handed stripping technique and a hand-over-hand retrieve that uses both hands. Since the double-handed rods tend to be heavier than any of their single-handed counterparts, a good deal of the time when fishing with the longer sticks I opt for a two-handed retrieve. Over time, tucking the rod under the armpit of your casting arm and retrieving line by means of a hand-over-hand stripping technique is less physically taxing than holding the rod in one hand and retrieving line with the free hand.

To be precise, even stripping line with the traditional single-handed method involves both hands because the finger (or fingers) of the rod hand is used to trap line to the rod. The reason for doing so is to prevent the line from falling away every time you strip it in. To fail to do so would result in a total loss of line control. If a fish were to strike the fly, you wouldn't be able to establish a positive hook set.

The hand-over-hand technique affords maximum line control, but initially until you get used to it, tucking the rod under your armpit may seem a little awkward. Then there's the matter of striking a fish. Instead of using the rod, setting the hook is accomplished by tugging back on the line. For many this practice takes some getting used to, but it's a very effective technique for establishing a positive hook set. Due to their increased length, sweeping a double-handed rod sideways in a strip-strike technique will cause the fly to move a considerable distance. If the fish has missed the fly, sweeping it along with the rod could easily move the fly away from the fish's preferred strike zone. This is not likely to be the case when you're manipulating the fly with both hands. Additionally, where strong-pulling fish are involved (striped bass come to mind), there is less likelihood of incurring a nasty line burn on one of your fingers. Because line is not trapped to the rod, it can be allowed to easily and safely slip through your hands when a fish decides to make off with the fly.

When a fish strikes you can react instantly with the two-handed stripping technique because all you have to do is tighten your grip on the line. Often this increased resistance is all it takes to set the hook. For added insurance you can impart a couple of short, sharp tugs on the line. Once the fish is firmly hooked, the next step is to simply grab the rod from under your arm with your rod hand and begin playing the fish.

Playing a fish with a two-handed stick is a lot of fun because the increased length adds to the sensation you feel when a strong-pulling fish resists the bend established in the rod. In relatively shallow-water applications where a fish cannot dive into the depths, the two-handed rod's added length can help increase the resistance the fish has to pull against. You have to be careful not to dangerously add to this resistance by overtightening the reel's drag or applying too much pressure with your hands.

Particularly with the longer two-handed rods, keep in mind that when a strong fish is stripping line from the reel, a number of factors in addition to the reel's drag mechanism will increase tension on the class tippet, the weakest link in the system. First off, compared to standard fly lines, Skagit-type lines have relatively large diameters and this will create considerably more drag in the water than their smaller-diameter counterparts. In addition, as line is being pulled from the reel, the spool's diameter decreases and this increases drag tension because the radial distance between the spool axle and the remaining line also diminishes. Drag tension is also created as line is being pulled through the rod guides, and due to their added length, you can expect this to be more of a factor when playing fish on longer double-handed rods. It's not possible to convey these factors into a numerical index, but you do have to be aware of the increased tension that can result when playing fish with longer rods and larger-diameter fly lines.

Even with standard 9-foot rods, anglers on foot often experience difficulty in properly landing their catch. They try to bring the fish close at hand by raising the rod toward them. Often a deep bend forms in the tip section, and it's not uncommon to lose the fish and break the rod at the same time. The problem can be exacerbated with longer two-handed rods, but there's a method of simplifying the task. When the fish is pretty well played out and maybe only a rod length or two away, strip several feet of line from the reel and let it fall into your stripping basket or at your feet. Now bring the rod toward you and allow this loose line to slip out through the guides. Once the rod is vertical and nearly against your body, you can reach out and grasp the section of line hanging outside the rod tip and hand-line the fish to you. The rod will remain completely straight, avoiding the deep bend in the tip section that so often results in breakage.

Fished properly, double-handed rods do have their place in salt water, and regardless of the line size you opt for, when you do connect with a fish that elongated rod bend created by a fish heading for the horizon makes for an exhilarating experience.

6 Line Management Devices

Doug Lum from Oahu never goes without his stripping basket when wading the bonefish flats.

Two features that distinguish fly fishing from conventional and spinning tackle modes are that the line carries the fly and the reel plays no part in the cast. With conventional and spinning gear, it is the weight of the bait or lure that carries the line on the cast. Conversely, in fly casting the cast is effected by means of the fly line itself. During the cast the unrolling loop of fly line (the relatively heavily weighted head section of the line) carries the fly along for the ride. The heavier or more bulky the fly, the more difficult it is to cast because it negatively affects the aerodynamics of the fly line as it cuts through the air. Because the reel plays no part in the cast, the total length of line that is going to be cast must be stripped from the reel prior to making the cast. Since the line is no longer stored on the reel, it has to lie somewhere close to the angler's feet, and if particular care is not taken to manage all this free line, a multitude of problems will inevitably result. A second factor to consider is that after the cast is executed, the retrieve is made by hand; line is not wound back on the reel's spool, so once again it's going to fall somewhere in the vicinity of the angler's feet.

In over four decades of fly-fishing I can recall many situations where some type of line management device would have prevented a costly mishap caused by a line that tangled or fouled. At fly-fishing shows you can watch casting demonstrations conducted indoors where everything goes smoothly. But indoor casting is practically the only situation I can think of where you can get by without using some type of container to manage the line that is lying at your feet. However, from personal experience I can tell you that even under these conditions the surface has to be absolutely clutter-free, and you have to be careful that you or someone nearby doesn't stand on the line.

In realistic fishing situations such ideal, trouble-free conditions seldom if ever exist. If you fish on foot, you will almost never encounter a surface that is devoid of obstacles or debris waiting to foul your fly line. An object that is as innocuous as a small twig, a broken clamshell, or a strand of grass or seaweed can easily snag the line and wipe out your cast. Even if your line falls on obstacle-free water, you're still at a disadvantage because the surface tends to hold the line like a magnet. The resistance of the line as it is being pulled free from the water can shorten your casts by as much as 20 feet. Add the effect of current that can pull the line opposite the direction you are trying to cast to, and things get even worse.

Over the years anglers fishing on foot have developed methods to capture line in their hand. Some have even been known to hold coils between their lips. I definitely don't recommend the latter practice. First off, there can be health risks posed by water quality issues. If the water is contaminated, it only takes small droplets to cause you problems. Denture wearers could also suffer some costly mishaps. I had a friend who tried holding some excess line between his lips and he paid a dear price on an Alaskan outing that really put a damper on his trip. On the second day of a weeklong trip, when he shot line on the forward cast, the line in his mouth caught a tooth and he lost a full set of dentures. In addition to the dental bill he incurred back home, he missed out on the lodge's excellent cuisine and had to get by mostly with applesauce and peanut butter.

By far the best way to secure line that has been stripped from the reel, whether you are wading or fishing from a boat, is to have it drop in some sort

At first glance there may not seem to be a connection, but Doug Lum can testify that his use of a stripping basket enabled him to cast far enough to present his fly to this 10-pound-plus bonefish.

of container. The ones you wear around your waist are commonly referred to as stripping baskets. Containers used for this purpose on boats are designated as stripping buckets. Both types are commercially available, or you can easily make them yourself. Whatever course you choose, you will find them indispensable.

Fishing from a boat, even those craft designed for special use by fly fishers (e.g., flats skiffs), can also pose a host of challenges. Fly-fishing craft normally feature clean, obstacle-free casting platforms. But the wind can blow the line into places it shouldn't be (including overboard), and the factor of errant feet is a potential hazard that never seems to go away. I doubt there was or is a fly fisher who hasn't stepped on the line at one time or another. When possible I like fishing barefoot, but even without shoes oftentimes I cannot feel the line when I am standing on it. It's very irritating to make what otherwise would have been an excellent delivery only to have it suddenly cut short because a section of line is planted under your foot.

Fishing off Rhode Island some years back, I lost a rare opportunity with a bluefin tuna because I was inadvertently standing on a section of line when

Left: A stripping bucket like this would have given me a much better chance with that bluefin tuna. It keeps everything primed and ready to go even when the boat is underway.

Below: This larger container I'm using was especially useful fishing from a panga in Baja because I could remove it from my waist, place it between my legs, and drop line into it similar to what you can do with a stripping bucket.

A deep stripping basket is very useful when shooting long lengths of line with two-handed rods. This one is available from Sea Level Fly Fishing.

the fish took my fly. I was striper fishing with my friend and accomplished Connecticut fly fisher Larry Merly. I spotted tuna breaking the surface a few hundred yards from where we were drifting, and Larry immediately headed out to intercept the school. I was wearing a basket but took it off when I switched to a heavier 12-weight outfit for the bluefin. Because I was in a hurry to make a cast as soon as we slid in front of the fish, I didn't want to take the time to put it back on (we're talking seconds). This proved to be a very costly decision. I made the cast and started stripping line furiously when one of the brutes nailed the streamer. The line shot up from the deck with alarming speed, and then suddenly everything went slack. A small section of line was caught under my left foot and the tippet broke. Needless to say, this was a very sickening experience made all the worse because it could have easily been prevented had I taken the time to use the basket I was wearing only minutes before.

On flats-type skiffs with level decks, one solution for those who don't want to wear a stripping basket or use a bucket is a product from Carbon Marine called the LineLair. This is a 22-by-22-inch soft rubber stripping mat with flexible rubber projections that does an excellent job of containing line as it falls toward your feet. The first time I used one was in Naples, Florida, on Captain Roan Zumfelde's skiff. We were in the backcountry, the wind started to crank, and line was being blown off the deck. Roan dragged out the mat and there were no further problems.

A container can provide an added service by protecting your line from harmful agents like gasoline or bug spray. During a Mexico trip years ago, we were fishing from a skiff (panga) and my partner was doing fine without a basket, simply letting his line fall on deck. After an hour or so of fishing, he began to notice that the fly line coating was starting to peel off. The boat deck was clutter-free, and we couldn't determine what was causing his line to deteriorate. However, we soon began to smell the cause of his problem. Gasoline leaked on deck from one of the hoses, and it destroyed a line that was practically brand-new.

The more line you have out, the greater the probability that Murphy's Law will rear its ugly head. In this respect the increasing popularity of shooting heads and two-handed rods can exacerbate line management problems. The extended casts associated with these systems involves long sections of running line that have to be properly contained to minimize the occurrence of distance-robbing tangles.

There are containers on the market that are made specifically for fly fishers, or you can fashion your own. Two commercially available baskets I have experience with are Sea Level's Belly Bucket and the Linekurv stripping basket.

Unlike many of the baskets I've purchased over the years, neither of these is too small or too shallow. You don't want one where the line easily falls out with the slightest motion. The Belly Bucket is made of neoprene, and the Linekurv basket is plastic. These materials are better than mesh-type baskets. The latter may fold for easy storage, but their sides tend to collapse. When that happens the line falls in on itself and will not shoot cleanly out of the basket. Both the Belly Bucket and Linekurv are well-thought-out designs. They're curved along one side to conform to your waist, with wide adjustable belts with plastic buckles, and their bottoms have a series of cones that help reduce tangles. Sea Level's Bucket II travel model is ideal for use on skiffs and larger boats; and as the name implies, it can double as a luggage container.

Despite all their features and partly because I've been doing so long before stripping containers were commercially available, there are times when I prefer using baskets that I've made myself. I've used everything from dishpans to milk cartons. The fact that there is such a vast array of plastic and rubber containers designed for all sorts of uses is fortunate because you're bound to find something that can be easily adapted as a stripping basket to suit your particular needs. I haven't found one yet that is ideal for all the conditions you are likely to encounter, but they are so inexpensive to make (the total cost for all the materials shouldn't be more than $10), you can easily have several at your disposal.

If I had to limit myself to just one, it would be the ubiquitous plastic dishpan. I first started using one in the early '70s for wade fishing Long Island Sound. As is the case with many handmade items, over time I made a number of improvements. Using a basket with its standard perfectly smooth bottom is better than having no container at all, but the line will still tangle readily, especially when you make any movement. I liken it to linguini in a pasta bowl. The way to alleviate this is to insert a number of flexible spikes up through the bottom of the container.

Through trial and error I finally settled on plastic tie wraps. Similar to the ones made from strands of heavy monofilament, they are flexible and will bend slightly as line shoots up out of the basket. This helps prevent the fly line or running line from bunching up on itself. Think of them as a set of fingers gingerly directing the line on its route through the rod guides. They are available in various lengths and tensile strengths, and two size classes I found that work well in baskets are the 4-inch ties with a tensile strength of 18 pounds and the 5½-inch ties rated at 40 pounds. I like mine to be roughly 3½ to 4 inches long. If you have a longer-length tie wrap and cut it down to this size, be sure to burn the end with a lighter or candle to smooth it over. Cutting the tie wraps with a pair of dikes or heavy-duty scissors will leave a sharp edge that can puncture your palm if you hit one of them while stripping line.

For a dishpan that is approximately 14 by 12 inches and 5¾ inches deep, all that is needed is about six of these projections. Drill the appropriate number of holes using a drill bit small enough to allow a snug fit when you push the tie wrap through the two holes in the bottom of the basket. You can also use a heated nail for this. Turn the container upside down and push the plastic ties through the drilled holes. I used to glue the flattened box-shaped ends to the underside of the bottom of the basket, but I've found with a snug fit the ties will stay in place without any adhesive.

For wading waist deep I prefer a basket with no holes in the bottom so water doesn't start seeping in. In this case use an adhesive like GOOP to make a water-tight seal around the holes where the tie wraps are inserted. However, when surf fishing I definitely want drain holes in the bottom. Water can easily splash in, and you want it to empty as quickly as possible. A series of quarter-size drain holes in the bottom of the basket will allow water to escape fairly quickly.

To fasten the container around my waist, I use a length of bungee cord. Use the kind with hooks on either end. Drill two holes in the top lip of the container at each end of the container's backside. By positioning the bungee cord hooks in the rear top lip of the basket, in the event a wave smacks the front side of the basket head on (not an uncommon occurrence), the basket will simply flip up, which helps prevent it from filling with water. With the bungee cord you can arrange the basket any way you like. For example, while playing a fish you can turn it around to your back or simply undo one of the hooks and get completely free of the basket. You can wear the basket directly in front of you, which is best if you like to use a two-handed stripping technique, or turn it so it lies at your hip if you're executing forceful, one-handed retrieves. If you don't like the bungee setup, you can use a belt with a plastic buckle.

One problem I used to have with these rectangular-shaped baskets is their tendency to slope downward when you have it placed directly in front of you at your midsection, but my good friend Frank Chen came up with a clever fix. Frank is a true master with the doubled-handed rod, both overhead and Spey, and particularly when he's casting off the beach, he has a prodigious amount of running line in the basket. With the basket drooping downward, line can spill out or tangle more frequently. To ensure the basket remains level, Frank glues a section of foam insulating tubing along the backside of the basket. The same material is available in department stores that sell water toys. They come in different colors and are marketed as Swim Noodles.

Developed by casting master Frank Chen, the addition of a "noodle"-type foam buffer to the backside of the basket helps maintain it in an upright position against your waist.

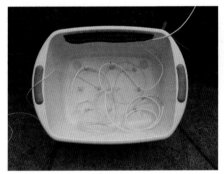 

A plastic dishpan with tie-wrap "fingers" makes for a very efficient stripping basket. The fingers help prevent the line from tangling in the basket.

I find the addition of plastic tie wraps to the cones in commercial baskets like this one from Linekurv can improve its line-handling functions.

When fishing beachfronts with high surf, I often switch to a plastic container intended to serve as a wastepaper basket. I find two sizes especially useful. There is a smaller version that measures 10 inches wide, 14½ inches long, and 15 inches deep. But for shooting head applications, particularly with double-handed rods where there is a substantial length of monofilament running line that has to be managed, I opt for a larger basket. Rubbermaid has a container that is rated as an 8-gallon bag size. It's 17 inches deep, 10 inches wide, and 14 inches across. Either of these baskets provides ample depth and width. The depth ensures that the line will remain in the basket even if you're running down the beach. The generous width makes it easy to strip line into the basket, and its flat sides allow you to position it comfortably against your hip or in front of your midsection.

When wading waist deep, it is best to have a basket with a solid bottom. If water seeps in, it will trap the line, impeding its travel up out of the basket, thereby decreasing your distance.

When traveling, the semirigid soft plastic and rubber baskets can serve a useful function when packing gear. They can easily be slipped into most soft luggage bags and then stuffed with all kinds of items like clothes and fishing gear. Even if the plastic tie wraps get bent in the process, they can easily be straightened with your fingers. Packed this way, the basket serves as a protective shield for fragile items that you don't want banged around.

There are those who find wearing a basket a bit uncomfortable or obtrusive, and too often they forgo its use. A common complaint among first-time users is that they pay too much attention trying to make sure the line they strip falls into the basket. But given a little time, most everyone readily adapts to one and it'll feel as natural as wearing a vest. True, they don't look very nice, but their advantages far outweigh their fashion flaws.

7

Knot So Fast

When you are fishing tooth-studded predators like this mako shark, you need to learn how to fasten fail-proof connections in both monofilament and wire.

My interest in knots dates back to my youthful experiences on Southern California party boats. The skippers on these boats live and die by the fish counts published in the newspapers. Anglers are more likely to ride the boats that consistently post the highest counts, and skippers become very upset when their clients needlessly lose fish due to improperly tied knots. These lessons were not lost on me, and ever since I've made it a practice to learn to properly tie the best connections for various functions. Some of my friends have taken offense,

There are times when you can connect with some large, strong-pulling fish in the surf. I was totally unprepared for this leopard shark that wore through my light tippet in less than a minute after it was hooked.

but I don't want anyone tying knots for me. If a knot fails (one telltale sign is sort of a pigtail curl at the tag end of the line), the responsibility is totally mine.

If you were to review the constantly growing literature devoted to fly fishing, one of the anomalies that might strike you is the fact that there is comparatively little written on the subject of knots. It's almost as if the topic were a footnote. You see a reference to it, but it's something the angling public generally isn't terribly interested in reading. From an author's perspective, it's not too easy to write about either. The subject tends to be technical and doesn't easily lend itself to the sort of prose readers are attracted to.

However, putting aside the interest factor, the subject of knots is one of the critical dimensions of our sport. You can be a very accomplished fly fisher equipped with the very best tackle components, but it all goes for naught if you suffer a knot failure. For anyone using a hook and line, a knot functions as the vital connection between angler and fish. And compared to anglers using spinning gear or conventional tackle setups, fly fishers typically have more connections to worry about. Backing must be connected to the reel's spool, then the fly line (or running line if you are using a shooting head) is connected to the backing (the running line must be connected to the shooting head), and finally the fly line itself will require some type of leader system.

There are a multitude of knots devoted solely to sport fishing, but it's only necessary to familiarize yourself with a few key connections used for tying on flies and connecting lines that differ in composition, diameter, and breaking strength. Bear in mind that several different knots may be used for the same function (e.g., connecting lines, tying on a fly, fastening a loop), but I will confine myself to those connections I've used over the years that have proven to be ideal for the task at hand. In my opinion the very best reference for these and a host of other useful knots for fly fishing is Lefty Kreh's *Fishing Knots* (Stackpole Books, 2007). Typical of his style, Lefty's instructions are clear and straightforward, and the illustrations are some of the best I've seen.

Aside from the one I made for myself (described in the Wire Loop Tool section), I haven't found it necessary to use any of the knot-tying tools you can buy. However, you do want a tool to cut line and trim your knots. For years I used regular nail clippers, but they are prone to rust and will get dull. One of the best commercial line clippers I've found is the Big Nippa by Rising. It has a nicely shaped thumb-control contour, a needle point you can poke through hook eyes to clear them of goop, and a hole in the top to which I tie a short section of old fly line or length of mono so I can quickly get hold of the tool when I need it.

Backing and Backing Connections

If you are assembling an outfit from scratch, the first connection involves attaching backing to the reel's spool. You basically have two choices for a backing line: Dacron or one of the newer gel-spun lines. I use both types, but there are a few qualities of gel-spun lines to be aware of. The principal advantage is their small diameter relative to high break strength, which allows you to spool a great deal of backing on the reel. I haven't calculated the difference, but the yardage you can wind on with 60-pound-test gel-spun compared to Dacron of the same break strength is significant. For this reason gel-spun has become the line of choice for blue-water fly fishers targeting the likes of tuna and billfish.

However, this small-diameter gel-spun also has a drawback: If you are not careful, under pressure it can cut you like a scalpel. Therefore, when winding this line on the spool, you should use some type of hand protection. Following a tip I learned from Stu Apte many years ago, I wear a thick cotton gardening glove. (I also use the glove when fighting large fish because I use my free hand to apply additional pressure on the line.) The line also has to be wound on the spool with sufficient tension. If the line isn't tight to the spool, it will dig into itself to a point where it cannot be pulled from the spool. This happened to a friend who was locked into a slug-fest with a big yellowfin tuna. The backing was not properly wound on the spool; it jammed and the sudden resistance caused the class tippet to break.

A good knot to use for attaching Dacron or gel-spun to the spool is a four-turn uni knot (also referred to as a Duncan loop). If you use a gel-spun line for backing, it's a good idea to take a section of duct tape and wrap it twice around the spool before tying on the line to help prevent the thin-diameter, slick line from slipping under pressure.

The Uni Knot

The uni knot was popularized by the famed Florida angler/writer Vic Dunaway. By mastering the simple method illustrated here, you can adapt it to various functions from tying on a fly to joining two sections of line together. Tied correctly it yields close to 100 percent breaking strength. When using the uni knot for tying on a fly, simply pass the tag end of the leader through the hook eye and follow the instructions. If you want a loop to allow the fly to swing more freely, pull on the main line until the wraps slide down toward the hook eye. When you have the desired size loop, pull on the tag end to tighten it. When a lot of pressure is exerted on the main line (as when playing a strong-pulling fish, for example), the wraps will slide down and snug against the hook eye.

Tying the Uni Knot

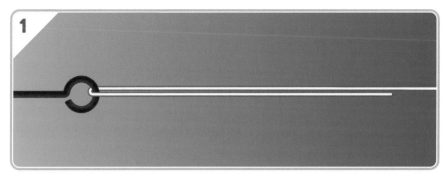

Take the tag end of the line and pass it around the reel's spool (a hook eye is illustrated because this knot can also be used to tie on a fly).

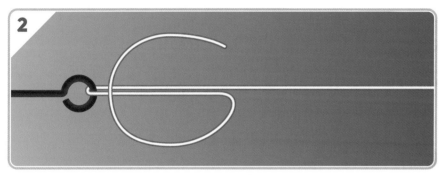

Pull the tag end toward the standing part of the line about 6 inches and then turn the tag end back away from the spool to form a loop.

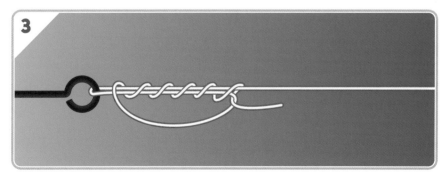

Take the tag end and pass it over the two legs of the loop, making four to six turns.

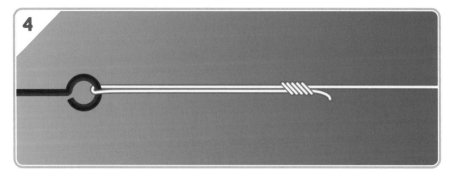

To tighten the coils, pull on the tag end.

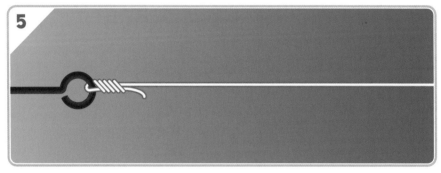

Pull on the main line and the knot will slide tight around the reel's spool, or hook eye if you are tying on a fly.

The Six-Turn Surgeon's Loop

At the tag end of the backing where I want to connect a fly line or shooting head running line, I also fashion a loop. For many years I used a Bimini twist to form this loop, but for the past several years I've switched to a six-turn surgeon's loop. (If you prefer tying a Bimini and are not sure how to go about it, I recommend the instructions in Lefty's book, *Fishing Knots*). To form the six-turn surgeon's loop, all you have to do is fold the line over itself to form the desired size loop and make a series of six overhand knots.

Tying the Six-Turn Surgeon's Knot

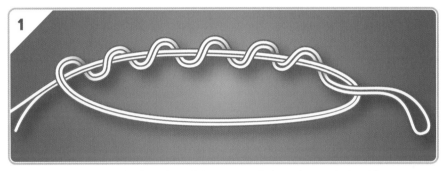

This is simply an extended version of the surgeon's loop. Instead of making two overhand turns of line through the loop, make six.

Moisten the knot and secure tightly.

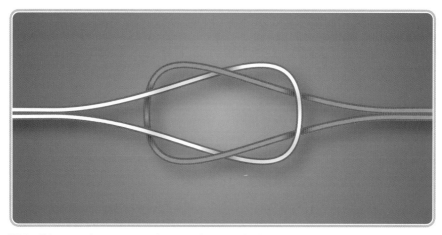

With all loop-to-loop connections, make sure the interconnected loops lie flat over each other prior to pulling the lines in the opposite direction to tighten. If one loop folds over the other, you have what amounts to a girth hitch, which can cut through the other loop.

To tighten this securely, I like to insert a screwdriver shaft inside the loop and pull on the main line with my other hand. Once again, wearing a glove or wrapping a thick cloth on the hand that is pulling on the standing part of the line is strongly recommended. The screwdriver inside the loop will help ensure that equal pressure is being applied to both legs of the line, and you don't have to worry about the line slicing through your palm or fingers.

This system of interlocking loops is the most efficient and one of the strongest means to make these connections. It also makes for quick and easy line changes; all you have to do is unlock the loops and slip one line (generally attached to a spool) through the other line's loop.

Fly Line Loops

Increasingly fly line manufacturers are offering lines with factory loops installed, but there will be times when you have to fashion your own. For example, on a full-length fly line, even with a preinstalled loop at the end that connects to the backing, I frequently cut off at least 20 feet or so of the running line section. About the only time I'm making 100-plus-foot casts with a line like this is during a casting demonstration at a fly-fishing show. For fishing purposes I normally do not need all this running line, and I eliminate a section of it to reduce the bulk of the fly line. This enables me to carry more backing on the reel. However, I still want an end loop in the running line section of the fly line to have a loop-to-loop connection with the backing. I also use a loop in the front end of the fly line to facilitate changing leaders and butt sections, and on some level sinking lines there is no factory loop so you will have to make your own. Contrary to some beliefs, a loop in the front end of a fly line where it joins the leader does not spook fish and it does not adversely affect the way the line turns over on the cast.

Particularly when fashioning loops the question of whether or not to use some type of glue is often raised. Lefty recommends working a drop of Loctite 406 (friends of mine have found this very difficult to procure) with a needle into a braided knot (Dacron or gel-spun) to ensure that the knot is as strong as the section of line with no knot in it. I never do so, and I've never experienced any knot failures. I always tighten and test a loop knot with something like a screwdriver blade. The only adhesive I sometimes use is of the rubber cement variety, and its sole purpose is merely to smooth the connection.

Wire Loop Tool

There are several different methods of fashioning loops in fly lines, and at one time or another I've used them all. But before we proceed I want to share a process of fashioning and using a very simple tool that will make some important connections a lot easier than you might expect. All you need is a piece of single-strand wire approximately 16 inches in length. To optimize the wire's usefulness in tying a variety of knots, it's important to select the right diameter. Too small of a diameter will cause the wire to kink easily and it won't be stiff enough to properly support a series of barrel wraps with monofilament leader material when tying a nail knot. After experimenting with a number of different sizes, I've found that diameters in the range of .016 to .018 work best. A wire diameter of .016 is designated as a number 6 with a breaking strength of about 61 pounds. Number 7 wire is .018 inch in diameter with a break strength of roughly 69 pounds.

Take the wire and bend it in half to form a loop that is approximately 8 inches in length. To help bend the wire to make the loop narrow, you can pinch down the V part of the bend with a pair of pliers. There are a number of ways to make the wire easy to locate when you need it and protect you from the sharp burrs at the tag ends that result from cutting the wire. The simplest method is to insert the two tag ends into a piece of foam. To secure it I use a few drops of superglue. You can also wrap the two tag ends with tape or glue them together with a dollop of hot glue from a glue gun. A more elaborate alternative was shown to me by Long Island fly fisher Neil Buchler whereby he crimps a sleeve on each of the two ends of the wire.

This is the author's simple wire knot-tying tool. The red foam at the tag end makes it easy to locate when you need it.

I originally made the tool mentioned here as a replacement for the splicing needle to make eye splices in hollow-core braids and Dacron. It is much more user-friendly and will generally last much longer than a splicing needle. The small angle of the bend makes it easy to work up inside the hollow-core braid or Dacron, and the added length of the wire makes for longer, more secure splices. Additionally, as we'll see, it's very useful for tying two varieties of nail knots.

I recommend making several of these wire loop tools so they are close at hand whenever you need one. Having one at your fly-tying desk or workbench and storing another in a tackle bag or box is a handy convenience.

Braided Loop Eye Splice

An eye splice makes for some slick end loops you can attach to the ends of fly lines and is especially useful for the larger-diameter fly lines like some of the heavier-weight floating and intermediate lines. As we will discuss in the section on speed nail knots, with relatively small-diameter fly lines it's easy to form an end loop by simply folding the line over itself and securing it with speed nail knots. However, with larger-diameter lines this would result in a bulge that might have difficulty passing through the rod guides. The alternative is to fashion a loop by means of a hollow-core monofilament or Dacron braid. Both are available in different breaking strengths and diameters. A 50-pound-test hollow-core monofilament braid will accommodate most large-diameter fly lines. To have a large enough diameter Dacron braid, you'll have to look for lines with break strengths in the 80- to 100-pound range.

With either line, begin the process with a 12-inch section of braid (if you want a larger loop, start with a longer length of braid). Insert the wire loop tool into the braid approximately 6 inches from the tag end.

Push the wire up inside the braid for a distance of about $1\frac{1}{2}$ inches. At this juncture push the wire out through the braid. Insert the tag end of the braid into the wire loop, then grasp the tag ends of the wire loop and pull the wire loop along with the tag end of the braid down through the same $1\frac{1}{2}$-inch section that you first ran the wire through. Pull the wire loop and the tag end out through the braid, leaving about a $\frac{1}{2}$-inch end loop in the other end of the braid.

It is common practice to insert the tag end into the braid a second time to ensure added security against it pulling out, but this is not really necessary. As long as the loop is pulled from dead center (and this is what happens with interlocking loops), the tag end will not pull free from the braid. But to make sure this will never occur, take the added step of tying a speed nail knot over the section of braid just below the juncture of the loop. Now regardless of how you pull on the loop, the one leg will not pull out.

Once you have formed the loop in the braid, the fly line must be worked into the remaining straight section of braid. With a $\frac{1}{2}$-inch loop in one end, there should be about 5 inches of single-strand braid remaining below the juncture of the loop. To make the job of working the fly line into this section of braid a bit easier, cut the tag end of the fly line on a bias. Now work it up inside the braid "inchworm style" by alternately pushing on the braid in one direction and then pushing on the fly line in the opposite direction, snaking the line through the braid's hollow core. Work the fly line all the way up through the braid until you reach the point where the tag end was pulled through. All that remains is to whip finish or nail knot the tag end of the braid where the fly line was initially inserted.

Braided Loop Eye Splice

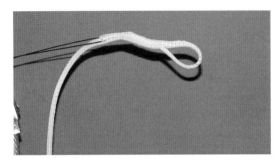

The wire loop tool is inserted into a hollow-core braid in preparation for forming an eye splice loop.

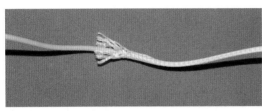

This shows a fly line being inserted into a length of hollow-core braid.

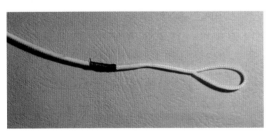

This is a completed eye splice loop attached to the front end of a fly line. The insertion point is whip finished with black fly-tying thread.

Braided Sleeve Connection

A section of hollow-core braid or Dacron can also be used to join two lines together. You simply insert the ends of the two lines you want to connect in each end of a 3- to 4-inch section of braid. When you pull the two lines apart, the braid tightens just like the Chinese finger grip you may have played with as a kid. Bind down the ends of the braid where you fed the line in by whip finishing with a bobbin and fly-tying thread or by means of a nail knot fashioned with small-diameter mono (10- or 12-pound test).

Nail Knot

The wire loop tool makes the nail knot easy to tie. The traditional method of tying this knot involves making barrel wraps around a section of line and a supporting base like a nail or tube (hence the name of the knot). The process of pushing the tag end of the line back under the wraps between the nail and the main line can be cumbersome, and over time the nail came to be replaced by a hollow tube. The tag end of the line of barrel wraps is inserted through the tube. The tube is then withdrawn, and you tighten the wraps by pulling on both ends the line. However, even if you use a fairly small-diameter tube (bear in mind that the diameter must be large enough to pass the line through), there still can be a relatively large gap between the wraps and the main line you are wrapping the line around. This gap can make it difficult to properly seat the knot in the final tightening process.

You don't have this problem when you wrap over the wire loop because the diameter is so small. After taking the desired number of turns around the wire loop and fly line (generally six to eight wraps), all you do is insert the tag end of the line through the wire loop and pull it under the wraps. There is very little gap remaining between the wraps and the fly line, so the knot is easily tightened.

Tying the Nail Knot with the Wire Loop Tool

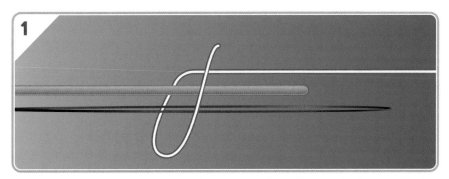

Lay the light mono that will serve as the nail knot alongside the wire loop and fly line with the loop's end facing to your right. Make the first wrap around the wire loop and fly line.

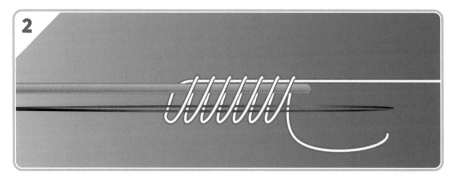

Continue wrapping to the right toward the end of the wire loop. Make six to eight wraps.

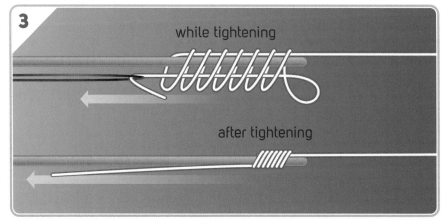

Insert the tag end of the mono you were wrapping with into the wire loop. Pull the wire loop to the left, make sure the wraps snug up tight together, and tighten by pulling on the tag and main line ends of the mono.

About the only time I use this method of tying a nail knot is when the knot is fashioned in a section of the fly line that is too great a distance from the tag end to make tying a speed nail knot practical. As discussed in the fly line chapter, you can use a monofilament nail knot to mark a continuous-length line at the point where there is sufficient line outside the rod tip to cast the fly with no time-consuming false casts (just one backcast followed by a final forward cast).

Speed Nail Knot

With relatively small-diameter fly lines, which is typically the case with sinking lines, I primarily use a speed nail knot to fashion end loops in the line. Simply fold the tag end of the fly line over itself to form the desired size loop (generally ¾ inch is ideal). Bind the two line sections together with two speed nail knots.

I first learned about the speed nail knot from Lefty Kreh, who is credited with popularizing this very useful knot. Many years ago in Long Beach, California, he was giving a presentation on rigging techniques where he demonstrated the traditional method of tying the nail knot. Lefty told me that after his demonstration, a young lad in the back of the room raised his hand. Lefty immediately acknowledged the youngster for what he thought would be a question, and was surprised when the boy, with just a tad hesitation, claimed that he had a faster way of tying the knot. Lefty had the kid come up to the table and tie what it is now referred to as the speed nail knot.

The reason I like to use 10- to 12-pound-test mono for forming this fly line loop is because when tightened this relatively light mono bites easily into the fly line's coating and makes for a relatively small-diameter loop. If the fly line you are wrapping over is stiff enough, you can make neat barrel wraps around the two legs of fly line without having to use the wire loop tool as a base.

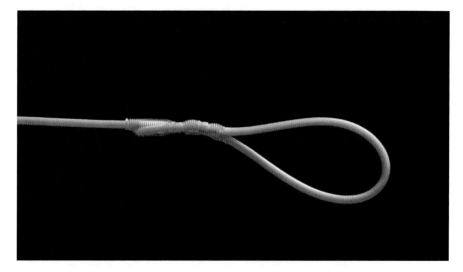

This is a fly line end loop formed by simply folding the line over itself to achieve the desired size loop. The two legs of line are bound together by means of two six- to eight-turn mono speed nail knots. The third series of wraps to the left of the two nail knots is an extended turn nail knot (10 to 15 turns) used to smooth the loop's tag end to prevent the connection from hanging up in the rod guides.

Tying the Speed Nail Knot with the Wire Loop Tool

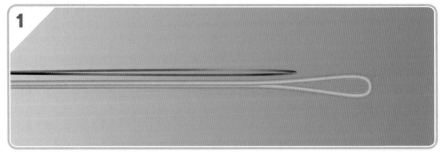

Place the wire loop tool alongside the rear section of the two legs of the fly line's loop.

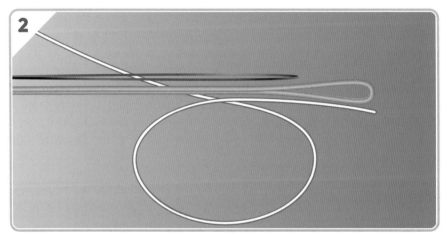

Form a loop in the 10- to 12-pound-test mono you are using to bind the legs of the fly line loop together. One tag end of this loop faces to the right and the other to the left. If you are right-handed, pinch everything together between the thumb and forefinger of your left hand.

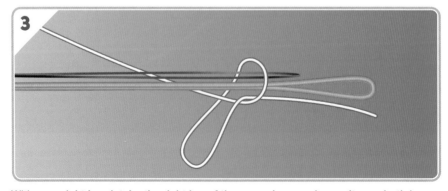

With your right hand, take the right leg of the mono loop and wrap it over both legs of the fly line and wire tool. Make sure the first crossover is to the left.

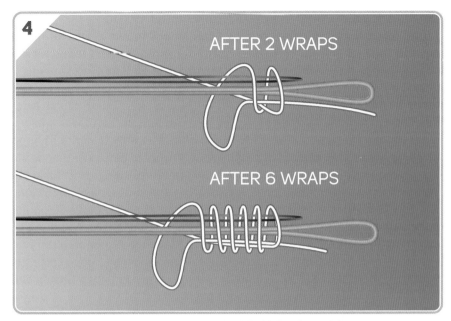

4

AFTER 2 WRAPS

AFTER 6 WRAPS

Continue wrapping the mono working to the left. Make six to eight wraps.

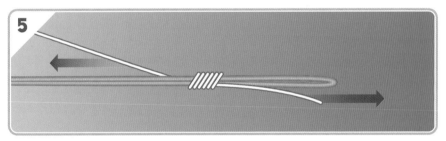

5

While continuing to hold the wraps in place with the thumb and forefinger of your left hand, grasp the right tag end of the mono loop's leg with your right hand and pull it to your right. This will cause the series of wraps to snug up flush with each other. To completely tighten the wraps, pull on the left and right tag ends of the mono loop.

To taper the tag end of the fly line loop, I use a third nail knot, taking as many as 12 to 15 turns. It's easy to keep all these barrel wraps uniform if you make the turns over the wire loop. With all these wraps the mono doesn't seat as securely as when you make only six to eight turns, but knot strength isn't the issue here. All you want to do is cover the tag end butt of the fly line loop with a smooth taper.

Using Mono to Form a Fly Line End Loop

A third method of fashioning a fly line end loop is to use a piece of heavy mono as the loop material. The first time I did so was when I found myself having to make an emergency fly line loop on a trip off Baja. I was tuna fishing and a yellowfin that I couldn't quite control ran under the boat, severing the fly line as it sawed across the keel. I was in a skiff, I didn't have extra lines close at hand (a mistake I resolved never to repeat), and I was anxious to get back in the action as quickly as possible. The only material I had to refashion a loop was monofilament line, and it worked perfectly. Practically any good-quality leader material in the 50-pound-test range will make an effective loop, and over the years I've found they generally tend to last as long as the fly line. All you need do is form the desired size loop in the 50-pound monofilament and bind it to the tag end of the fly line with nail knots. The only thing I do differently when using mono for a loop as opposed to braid is to make four or five speed nail knots to the monofilament loop legs to the fly line. To make the loop as smooth as possible, you can flatten the tag end sections of the monofilament loop with pliers.

When fashioning a mono loop to a clear intermediate line, I like to use 15-pound-test monofilament to tie the nail knots. Intermediate lines do not have coatings like the other fly lines, so the heavier monofilament for the nail knots is needed to achieve a superstrong binding effect. Again, when properly tied, you should never have one of these loops pull free. I have put these loops over my shoe and pulled on the fly line with both hands. The fly line has broken, the monofilament loop broke once, but never has the loop itself pulled free from the fly line.

Follow the Leader

The section of line that immediately follows the fly line is the leader. During the cast the fly line unrolls, and it's the leader's function to turn over the fly and have it unfold without collapsing in a heap on the water. Some advocate that a relatively long, tapered leader is necessary to achieve a proper presentation, but in reality the type of leader you construct should be a function of the particular set of conditions you have to contend with. For clear, shallow water applications where you're sight-fishing, long leaders in the 9- to 14-foot range may be required. In contrast, for deeper water blind-casting situations, the leader can be considerably shorter, maybe only 5 or 6 feet long, and, as we'll see, sometimes even shorter than that.

For most inshore applications (and that is the setting for most saltwater fly fishing), I generally use two and sometimes three leader sections. The portion that normally connects directly to the fly line is referred to as the butt section, and to ensure the fly turns over correctly at the completion of the cast, it should make up roughly half the length of the leader system. For example, if you plan to fish a 10-foot leader for bonefish, the butt section should be about 5 feet in length.

Compared to the class tippet, standard practice dictates that the butt section be composed of relatively heavy mono. Thus for 8- to 10-weight fly lines, a butt section of 30- to 40-pound-test mono is appropriate. For big-game applications, I step up to a 50- or 60-pound-test butt section. This heavier and correspondingly larger-diameter section of mono can help withstand the abrasive effects of fish such as large tarpon, billfish, and sharks.

Calico, or kelp, bass are a popular West Coast inshore species. They usually feed down in the water column and are not leader shy, which means that the length can be kept relatively short, 5 to 6 feet.

I fasten the butt section to the fly line or shooting head via a loop-to-loop connection. Simply tie a surgeon's loop in the butt leader and loop it through the fly line's loop. Normally I tie a surgeon's loop in the other end of the butt section leader to connect it to an end loop in a class tippet.

When I first started fly fishing, two things that were constantly drummed into me was that a butt section was absolutely necessary and that it must be constructed of the stiffest monofilament you could find. These proved to be pure myths. The fact is, a butt section is not always necessary, and there are many instances where it is perfectly suitable to connect the tippet (the class tippet, according to IGFA nomenclature) directly to the tag end of the fly line and tie the fly to the tag end of the tippet. This is often the case with fishing sinking lines, where you want the fly to get down as quickly as possible. A shorter leader (3 feet or so) will tend to ride at the same level as a sinking line, whereas a long leader will tend to develop a bow, slowing the fly's descent. With a proper casting stroke, there is no negative effect on the fly's delivery.

The second bit of misinformation about the necessity of a very stiff butt section really doesn't make sense when you think about how a fly line unfolds during its flight path. Instead of being stiff, the butt section should be flexible. If it's too stiff, the fly will not turn over properly at the conclusion of the forward cast, and this is readily demonstrated in cases where a wire-leader bite tippet (sometimes referred to as a shock leader) is being used. IGFA regulations allow the use of any material (mono, single-strand wire, braided wire) as a bite tippet but it cannot exceed 12 inches in total length, including any connecting knots. But with wire, even this 12-inch length can make it difficult to turn over the fly, so even though insurance against being bitten off by a toothy predator may be considerably reduced, in situations where relatively long casts are necessary for the sake of proper fly delivery, I often shorten the wire to 5 or 6 inches.

With all the connections in the leader system, take care to be mindful of the weak link principle. A chain is only as strong as its weakest link, and in a multi-section leader the leader is only as strong as the weakest section of line, which is normally the class tippet. The objective therefore is to ensure that all the knots connecting the different sections of leader will yield 100 percent of the rated breaking strength of the class tippet. For example, if you want to connect a length of 12-pound-test line to a section of 30-pound-test line, the object is to tie a knot that will not compromise the rated breaking strength of the lighter 12-pound test. Recall that with fly-fishing leaders the class tippet according to IGFA standards ranges from 2- to 20-pound test. To ensure the integrity of the total rated breaking strength of the class tippet, it is necessary that all connections be tied with knots that do not weaken it in any way.

This means that when using a butt section, the first concern is to form a connection with the lighter class tippet that will not weaken the tippet's rated break strength. To preserve the class tippet's break strength, I recommend tying either a Bimini twist or six turn surgeon's loop in the tippet and using the resulting loop for a number of different connection options to the butt section. The method I generally opt for is a loop-to-loop connection. I double the class tippet loop that was formed by a Bimini or six-turn surgeon's knot and then simply tie a surgeon's knot (loop) in the doubled loop. This yields a loop that has two strands of line instead of just one. Then I interlock this double-line loop to the surgeon's loop in the tag end of the butt section. The double-line loop ensures that the larger-diameter butt section will not wear through the smaller-diameter class tippet. In addition, when I want to change the class tippet, all I have to do is unlock the loops without having to cut any line. Similarly, if you need to use a monofilament bite leader, a Bimini or six-turn surgeon's will also have to be tied in the other end of the class tippet to use for a variety of connections with the terminal leader.

The Albright knot and the so-called Huffnagle are examples of 100 percent knots that utilize the loop in the class tippet formed from the Bimini or six-turn surgeon's as the basis for tying it to a heavier section of monofilament leader.

Tying the Albright Knot

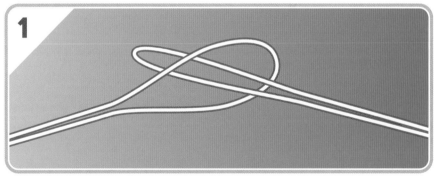

Bend the bite tippet material over itself to form a loop. Take the loop formed in the class tippet and push it through the bite leader loop.

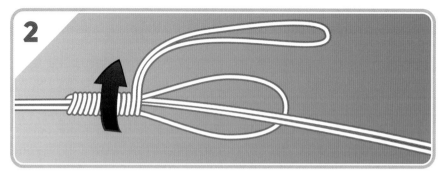

Take the class tippet loop and make 8 to 10 wraps around both legs of the bite leader loop. Make the wraps working to your right.

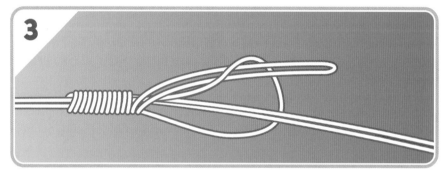

With the last wrap push the tag end through the bite tippet loop. Be sure the class tippet loop goes through the bite tippet loop the same way it entered.

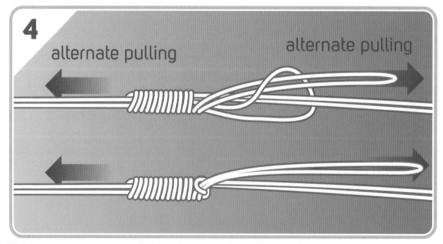

Tighten the wraps by carefully and alternately pulling on the class tippet loop and the standing part of the bite leader.

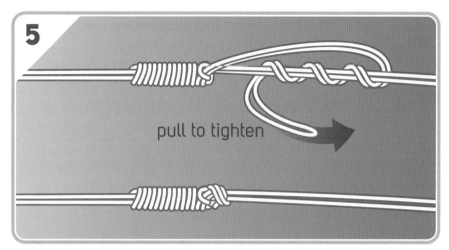

When the wraps are snug against the end of the bite leader, to lock the knot make three half hitches around the bite leader's main line and pull it tight. Trim the two tag ends of the remaining class tippet loop.

If there is not a great deal of difference in the diameter of the two lines you want to join—for example, tying a 12- or 16-pound-test class tippet to a 30-pound-test bite leader—I've found that a three-turn surgeon's knot makes for a quick and very secure connection. All you have to is overlap the two lines for a foot or so and tie three overhand knots with the double lines. Just be sure all four legs of the overlapping sections pull up evenly when tightening the knot.

Tying the Huffnagle Knot

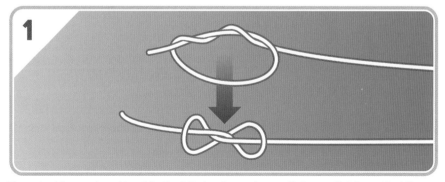

Tie a double overhand knot in the bite leader and snug it down slightly so that it forms what looks like a figure eight. This forms two small end loops.

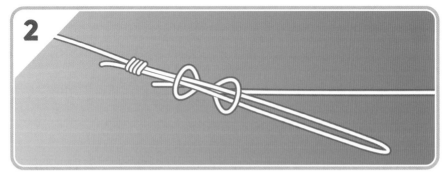

Pass the class tippet's loop through both these loops.

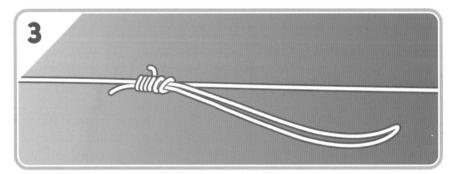

Tighten the bite leader's double overhand, effectively closing its two small loops.

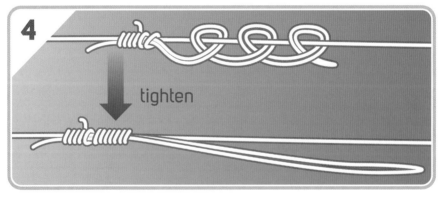

Make three half hitches around the bite leader with the class tippet loop and snug each of these tight.

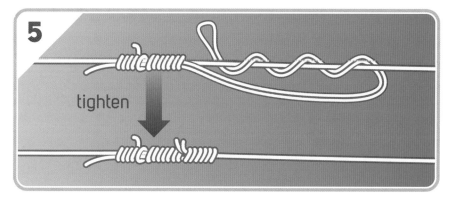

5

tighten

With the remaining section of the class tippet's loop, take four to six turns around the bite leader and snug this tight against the last half hitch. Trim all the tag ends.

In those instances where you forgo the use of a butt section, the class tippet is connected directly to the fly line via a loop-to-loop connection. You'll need an end loop in the class tippet to do so, and to form this I recommend the aforementioned Bimini twist or a six-turn surgeon's loop knot. Once this loop is formed, I fold it over itself to form a two-leg loop that I interlock to the fly line loop.

Doing the Twist

There is a second method of attaching a class tippet directly to a fly line that I learned from Brandon Powers. I remember we were taking a break at a fly show in Louisiana, and Brandon was watching me tie some leaders in preparation for an upcoming redfish trip. He offered to show me a method of doubling a section of the class tippet to connect to the end loop in the fly line. It involves twisting a portion of the leader that is similar to what I do with the loop that is formed from a Bimini or six-turn surgeon's.

Because it is doubled over and twisted, this section of the line has a break strength double that of the single strand. The effect is similar to what you would achieve by joining the class tippet to a butt section, only here you are using only the class tippet and the resulting double-strand twisted loop interlocks securely with the fly line's end loop.

As stated above, this doubled section can serve as a substitute for a butt section so all you have is a single tippet section with no interconnections. An added plus is that the twisted portion will stretch under pressure. Insert your finger, or better yet something like a pen or screwdriver, into the twisted loop and pull on the untwisted section of line, and you'll see and feel the effect. This can provide an extra margin of error if you apply a lot of pressure on a fish, particularly when using light tippets like 8- or 10-pound test.

Tying the Twisted Leader

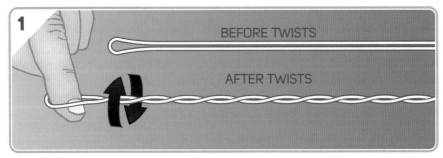

Depending on the length of the class tippet you want, take a section of the line and fold it over itself to form a loop. For most purposes I form a loop that is approximately 3 feet long. Stretch the leader before you begin twisting it so it lies nice and straight. Insert your finger into the loop and begin making a series of counterclockwise twists (about 10 or so) by rotating your hand.

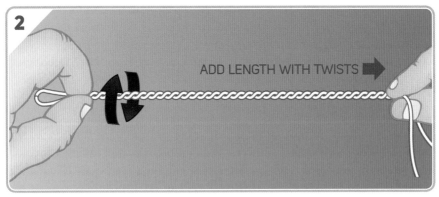

Pinch the top portion of the column of twists between your thumb and forefinger (I do so with my left hand). With your other hand (my right), hold the two legs of the untwisted line between your thumb and forefinger. Continue lengthening the column of twists by pushing the thumb of your left hand upwards against the surface of your forefinger. This causes the strands to crisscross one another. The trick is to allow the line to slip between the two fingers of your right hand as you form the twists with your left thumb and forefinger.

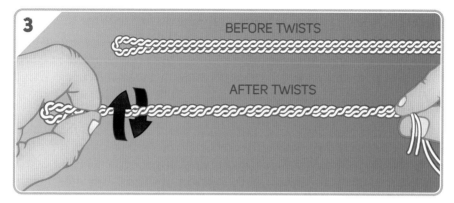

When there is approximately 20 inches (this may vary) of twisted leader, fold the twisted section over itself to form a loop. I used to tie a surgeon's knot at the end of the twists to secure it, but this isn't necessary. The twists will remain in place. Begin forming a second column of twists directly over the first twisted column using the same method you did to form the first series of twists. I like to make this second column of twists roughly 1½ feet in length, but you can vary the length to adjust to your fishing conditions.

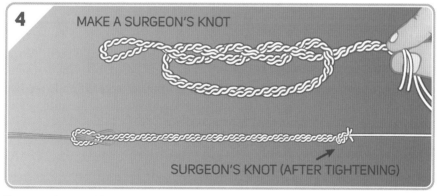

Once you have achieved the desired length, tie a surgeon's knot at the end of these twists to yield a surgeon's loop at the end of the double twists. This double-twisted section of line makes for an incredibly strong class tippet section, and you have only used one section of line.

Connecting the Fly

When tying a fly directly to the tag end of the class tippet, I use one of three connections: a nonslip loop, a Palomar knot, or a fisherman's knot.

As its name implies, the nonslip loop knot yields a loop that allows the fly to swing freely during the retrieve or when it's drifting with the current. The result is that the fly tends to be more active and therefore supposedly more attractive to fish. I don't know of anyone who has kept accurate records to verify that this is indeed the case. Recounting my own experiences, I cannot report any dramatic differences in the number of strikes elicited fishing the identical fly for the same species under the same conditions but using a knot other than the nonslip loop. If you feel fish will be more attracted to your fly by virtue of a loop connection, by all means use one. I do for much of my inshore fishing because the argument makes sense and I like the way the fly moves in the water, but I have nothing to confirm that it's more effective. You could also use the uni knot, but as mentioned earlier under sufficient pressure this knot will slide tight against the hook eye. For that reason I prefer the nonslip loop.

Oftentimes I tie on a fly with connections that have stood the test of time, long before the popularity of loop knots. In all my years of fishing conventional gear, particularly under the challenging conditions of long-range trips where big fish are fought from a stand-up position without benefit of the boat chasing down the fish, two knots that never failed were the Palomar and the so called fisherman's knot. These are knots that seat tightly against the hook eye and when tied carefully, like the nonslip loop, are rated close to 100 percent of the line's rated break strength.

Tying the Nonslip Loop Knot

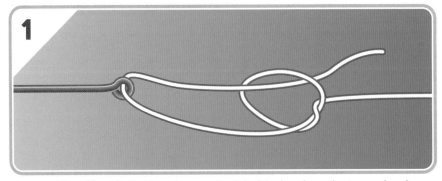

Tie an overhand knot in the tippet approximately 6 inches from the tag end and pass the tag end through the hook eye and back through the overhand knot. You can alter the size of the loop by reducing the size of the overhand knot and working it toward the hook eye. I find a loop size of roughly ¼ inch is ideal for most conditions.

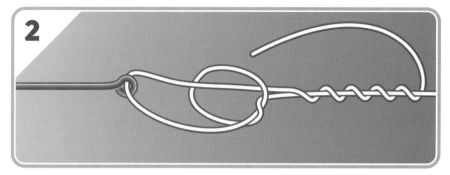

Make a series of wraps around the standing part of the line. The number of wraps is determined by the breaking strength of your tippet. For example, with 8- to 10-pound-test tippets, make five wraps; with 16- and 20-pound tippets, four are sufficient.

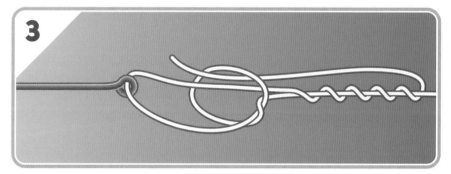

Pass the tag end back through the overhand knot, making sure it goes through the same way it first entered.

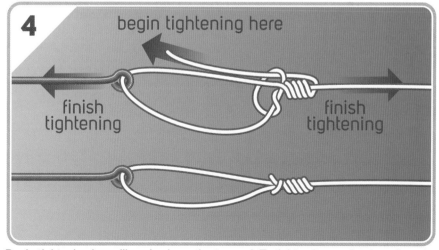

Begin tightening by pulling slowly on the tag end. To tighten it completely, pull on the fly (it's a good idea to use something other than your fingers) and the standing part of the tippet.

Tying the Palomar Knot

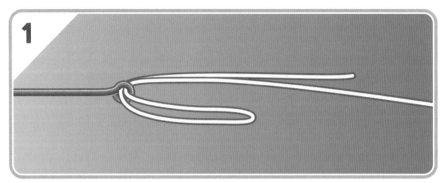

1

One of the attributes I like about this knot is that it affords an extra measure of safety by having two strands of the leader pass through the hook eye. To form these double strands, make a loop in the leader (I like about 7 inches to work with) and pass it through the hook eye.

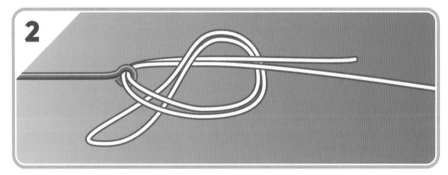

2

Take this loop and tie an overhand knot with it around the standing part of the leader.

3

fly passes through the loop

Pass the fly through the remaining loop in the tippet.

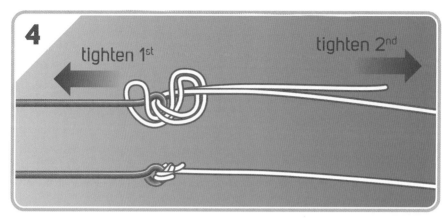

Begin tightening the knot by slowly pulling on the standing part of the leader. As the knot begins to close, pull on the tag end of the loop. Trim the tag end.

Tying the Fisherman's Knot

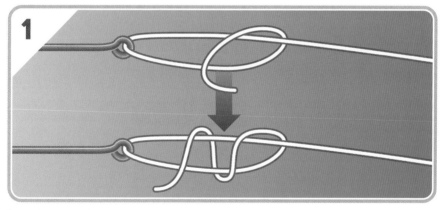

Pass the tag end of the leader through the hook eye, fold it back toward the opposite standing part of the line (toward the hook eye), and begin making wraps around the double section of line.

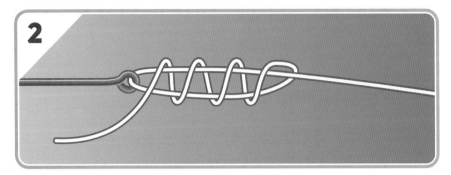

For leaders under 20-pound test, make five wraps; with lines heavier than that, all you need is three.

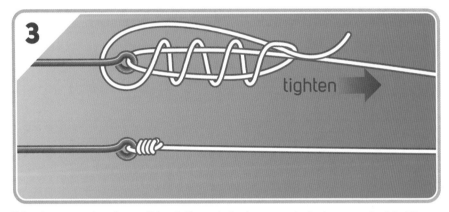

Take the tag end and pass it back through the loop created when you doubled the line back on itself. Slowly but firmly pull on the standing part of the line to seat the knot firmly against the hook eye.

Attaching the Fly to the Bite Tippet

The one connection where you do not have to be concerned with a 100 percent breaking strength is where the fly is tied to the tag end of a bite tippet. By their nature these bite tippets typically have high-rated breaking strengths. That is the reason they are being used in the first place. Higher breaking strengths are associated with increased line thickness, and this helps prevent break-offs by guarding against teeth, scales, and all matter of abrasive factors that can quickly wear through a line. The point is, if the bite leader has a breaking strength that is at least twice that of the class tippet, you can tie the fly on with a knot that has comparatively low breaking strength because it still will not jeopardize the integrity of the class tippet.

For example, imagine you are using a knot like some of the ones I am about to describe that may be rated at only 50 or 60 percent breaking strength. A simple overhand knot is a perfect illustration. The knot cuts into itself and can reduce the rated breaking strength of a line by as much as 50 percent. With a bite tippet that is rated let's say at 60-pound test, tying an overhand knot could reduce the break strength to 30 pounds. But even if you are using the heaviest IGFA-rated class tippet, which is 20-pound test, you still have a large insurance hedge because the compromised bite leader connection would still yield 10 more pounds breaking strength. So here we don't have to worry about the principle of the weak link.

Clifford's Knot

The first knot I want to describe for tying a fly to a bite tippet is one that Lefty Kreh and I learned about many years ago when we were fishing at Casa Mar in Costa Rica. One of the guides at the time was a young man named Clifford, and he showed us a knot that Lefty later appropriately referred to as Clifford's knot. I first described it in my book *Baja on the Fly* and use it often for tying flies on bite leaders for a variety of species.

One of the unique features of this knot, which is essentially a simplified version of a bowline, is the fact that it can be loosened, completely undone, and retied repeatedly for changing flies without ever having to cut the line. A second feature of this knot is that like the nonslip loop, the tag end faces downward toward the hook eye. This means that there is less chance for debris like sea grass to foul on this remaining nub of line.

Tying Clifford's Knot

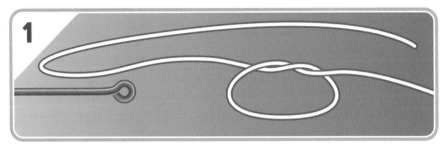

As in the other two knots I will describe, Clifford's knot begins with an overhand knot tied in the main section of line approximately 6 or 7 inches from the tag end. Leave a small circle but do not tighten it.

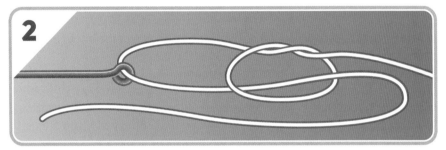

Pass the tag end of the bite tippet through the hook eye and then bring it through the center of the overhand knot.

Take the tag end and bring it behind the standing part of the line and reenter the circle of the overhand knot.

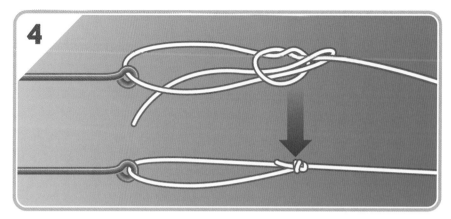

Tighten the resulting loop by grasping the fly in one hand and pulling on the standing part of the line with the other hand.

Nonslip Loop Knot Variation

The second knot is a modification I make to the nonslip loop knot. Tie the overhand knot in the main section of line, pass the tag end through the hook eye, and bring it back through the overhand knot. But instead of making the recommended four or more turns around the standing part of the line, with heavy bite leader material all you need is a minimum of three turns. After making the wraps, pass the tag end through the overhand, once again exiting on the same side of the circle where the line was first passed through. Pull slowly on the tag end to begin tightening the wraps. To seat the wraps firmly, pull on the standing part of the line and the fly in opposite directions.

Ted's Knot

The third knot in this series is one I learned about from Ted Juracsik. Ted, of course, is recognized for his premier fly reels, but what a lot of people may not know is that he spends a tremendous amount of time on the water fishing from his home base in Chokoloskee, Florida. Some time ago when he was poling me along one of his favorite spots searching for tarpon that had slid into the mangroves, I started to tie on a different fly. He asked me to wait because he had a knot he wanted to show me. Of all the knots I've tried for tying on flies to bite tippets, I find this one by far the easiest and quickest to tie. Ted said he didn't develop it and has used it for over 20 years but cannot recall who first showed it to him. For lack of a better term, I refer to it as Ted's knot.

Tying Ted's Knot

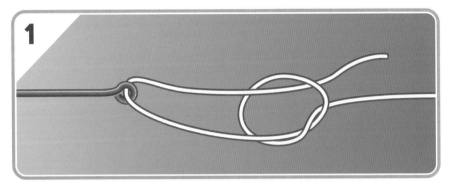

Begin by tying an overhand knot in the main section of line. Pass the tag end through the hook eye and back through the circle formed by the overhand knot.

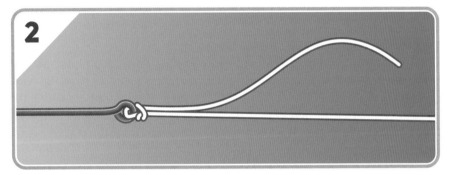

Tighten the overhand knot, making it snug against the hook eye.

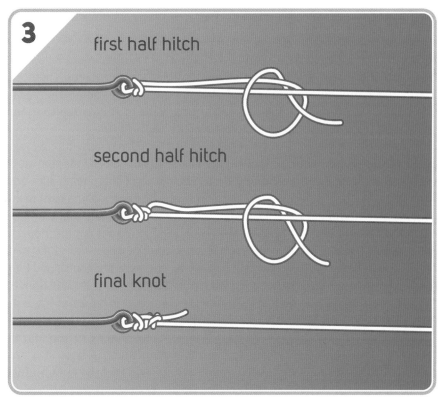

3

first half hitch

second half hitch

final knot

Make two half hitches around the standing part. As in all these bite tippet knots, it's best to grasp the hook portion of the fly with pliers and pull on the leader to get the knot really snug. The tightened knot will leave a very small loop at the hook eye that like the other two knots will permit the fly to swing at the end of the leader.

Wire Bite Tippets

For all the years I spent fishing areas like Southern California and Baja, wire was (and still is) an integral part of my terminal tackle system. Offshore, sharks (primarily blues and makos) made for exciting fly rod action. Today this remains a productive fishery, and if you want to stay connected and enjoy the fun, wire bite tippets are an absolute necessity.

In the early '70s when I was a regular on the San Diego–based long-range circuit, "More wire!" was a familiar cry. The seagoing speedsters that were the object of these directives were wahoo. Their scalpel-sharp teeth slice and sever like a master sushi chef. In those days I was the only one on board using fly gear, and after logging many 16-day trips, I was fortunate enough to land a handful of these highly prized gamesters on the fly. Were it not for properly tied wire bite leaders, these catches would have never been possible. Likewise, other popular game fish like bluefish, barracuda, sharks, and Spanish and king mackerel would never have been landed had it not been for wire bite tippets.

In the early days you had to fashion your own, and for most of my wire needs I still do, but today there are alternatives like a wire product from Aquateko called Knot 2 Kinky. Perhaps the most outstanding feature of this relatively small-diameter wire is the fact that you can tie a knot in it and connect it directly to a fly, just like you would with a heavy mono bite tippet. The wire also has a stretch factor (15 to 20 percent) that affords an extra margin of safety, making it possible to use lighter wire than normally would be advisable with single-strand wire. For most inshore applications, I recommend their 25- and 45-pound-test wire.

If you want to make your own, I recommend using single-strand wire. A size that I find works well for practically all my fly-fishing needs is one with a .018 diameter and a breaking strength of approximately 69-pound test. This diameter size presents a fairly slim profile and is easy to work with. If curls begin to form after catching a few fish, most can be straightened by hand (another plus for the Knot 2 Kinky wire is that it is very kink resistant).

As with any bite leader, there are two connections you have to contend with. The first involves tying the wire to the fly. The second is joining the wire to the mono class tippet. There are several ways to effect this. To facilitate quick fly changes, some anglers like to connect one end of the wire to a snap. Personally I do not like the extra hardware and the bulky profile. The haywire twist, which I'm about to discuss, is a neat, simple alternative. The second tying process, the wire-to-mono connection, is one that many fly fishers find troublesome. Instead of tying the wire directly to the mono, an alternative I favor is to use a small barrel swivel. The mono class tippet is tied to one ring of the swivel, with the wire fastened to the other ring. I have tied all my wahoo leaders this way and have never experienced any failures.

As functional as wire is when fishing tooth-studded predators, it's not without a downside. One dysfunction was alluded to when we discussed the problem of using too stiff a butt section. Due to wire's inherent stiffness, it can impair the fly's ability to turn over properly at the conclusion of the forward cast. For that reason when relatively long casts are necessary, it's best to use the shortest length wire bite tippet possible. I generally try to keep mine to within 5 inches and haven't lost many fish with this abbreviated length.

More troublesome is the fact that wire can turn off fish. Southern California–based barracuda are a good example. Though not as formidable as their tropical cousins, they do have cutting teeth that can quickly sever a monofilament leader. But you will find that you will elicit far more strikes if you forgo wire and tie the fly directly to the class tippet. Tying flies on long-shank hooks can partially guard against being prematurely bit off. I have experienced the same effect with yellowfin tuna. Yellowfin, particularly the larger specimens, can wear through smaller-diameter monofilament. Wire bite tippets will prevent this, but there have been too many instances where I discovered that I drew far more strikes with mono. Even relatively large-diameter mono like 50-pound test does not seem to be as obtrusive as wire.

Here is an important tip for finishing the haywire twist: To remove the remaining tag end flush to the last barrel wrap, this small piece of wire must be broken off. If you simply nip it off with cutters, a sharp burr will be formed, which can easily slice your hand when grabbing the leader. Grasp the wire with the pliers at the juncture of the last barrel wrap. Position the wire in the jaws so that the tag end is extending out from the standing part of the wire pointing to your right. If need be, bend the tag end so that it forms a right angle to the barrel wraps. Now bend the tag end upward and make a slight backward twist in a clockwise direction. This should cause the wire to break off cleanly with only one or two rotations.

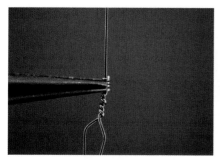

Grasp the wire with pliers at the juncture of the first barrel wrap.

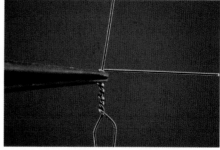

Position the wire so that the tag end is facing right. Bend this tag end upward with a slight twist backward to the left to make a clean break in the wire

Tying the Haywire Twist

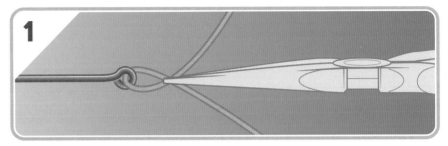

Unless you are blessed with very strong fingers, a pair of pliers is strongly recommended. Bend the wire to form a loop approximately 6 inches long. Grasp the loop with pliers and begin crisscrossing both legs of the loop. The key to this connection is forming three and half true Xs in the wire. The easiest and most effective way to achieve this is to crisscross the wire to form the first X and then hold this juncture between the pliers' jaws. With the crisscrossed wire held securely in place, spread the wire legs outward so they flare out in a wide V configuration.

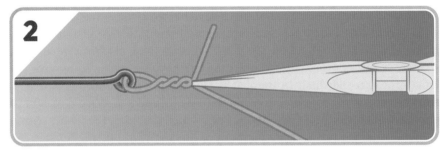

While holding the pliers in one hand, twist the two legs to form three more complete Xs. If you merely spiral one leg of the wire around the other, under pressure the wire could unravel. This will not happen if the wire is crisscrossed in an X pattern. When the third X is formed, reposition the pliers so the jaws are close to this last juncture.

Take the tag end of the wire and spiral it around the standing part, forming a series of four close barrel wraps.

The tag end of the wire is at a right angle to the standing part of the wire. To cleanly break off the tag, rotate it slightly to the left up and behind the wraps. Ideally it should only take one or two rotations to break it off.

8 Flies for Salt Water

Captain Roan Zumfelde's Hammerhead Jerk Bait is a good example of a novel weighted pattern.

n 1995 Lefty Kreh's book *Saltwater Fly Patterns* was a compilation of the major saltwater patterns in use at the time. I still consider it an excellent reference source, but since then the number of flies designated for saltwater use has grown dramatically. Fly selection can be a matter of endless debate, but part of the allure and challenge of this phase of the sport is that fly tying is in a constant state of evolution. Just when you think you have settled on a definitive pattern for your fishing needs, something else comes along that seems to work even better.

The "master" Bob Popovics using two of his favorite Renzetti vises to tie an elongated squid pattern.

Despite the fact that I've been at this for almost half a century, I rate my own fly-tying skills as modest at best. But in partial defense I can say that I tie flies to catch fish, not people's credit cards. Normally when someone who is invariably a far more talented tier gives me one of their flies to fish, I'm reluctant to use it.

My creations will never look anywhere as good as some of those who tie commercially or a host of other friends who are very talented at the vise, but I love the fly-tying process and I derive an extra measure of satisfaction taking a fish on something I created. However, I do not take this to the extreme of absolutely refusing to use someone else's flies, particularly if that person is a guide with intimate knowledge of the fishery. I always like to show guides the flies I've brought along and ask what they think I should tie on. But when it is clear that my flies are not producing and guides want me to try one of their patterns, I do so.

The bottom line is that I want to draw strikes, and if I don't have anything in my box that is doing the job, I'm very willing to try something different. I write this because friends who guide tell me frustrating tales of stubborn clients who steadfastly refuse to fish a fly they haven't tied and then complain about the poor fishing.

This backcountry tarpon pattern is from Captain Roan Zumfelde.

Aside from the accessibility factor, one of the reasons I never became heavily involved with trout fishing was the intricacy of the insect patterns I would see at some of the fishing shows. It seemed like you had to have the hands of a surgeon to tie a realistic pattern. Furthermore, simply in terms of size, it appeared that most saltwater patterns were easier to tie. With the freshwater fishing I most often gravitate toward, which includes the likes of largemouth and smallmouth bass, pickerel, and pike, where there is considerable room for many saltwater patterns I feel comfortable tying flies for these species. Bob Popovics, Ed Jaworowski, and I had the good fortune to experience three consecutive seasons of terrific pike fishing in Saskatchewan. On our first trip we weren't sure how our saltwater patterns would work on these fish, but in the first few minutes of wetting a line, we found that these flies proved to be the hot ticket.

In fact, it was on one of these trips that Bob developed his Weedless Bend-back Silicone fly. In some places we were fishing in water choked with lily pads. Prior to this trip, over the years I had used just about every weedless configuration ever devised. Wire weed guards, straight and bent at different angles, and single- and double-mono weed guards of varying diameter and

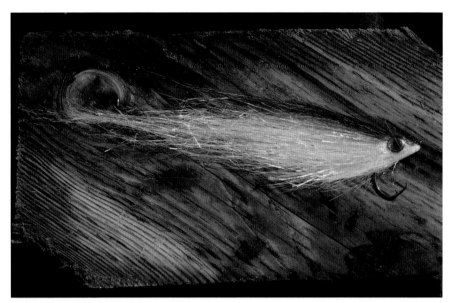

One of the saltwater patterns I used with good success is Bill and Kate Howe's FPF (Flashy Profile Fly), a streamer designed for offshore fishing. It is tied on a circle hook. With this hook style the object is not to strike the fish in the conventional manner by pulling back on the line. Instead, when you feel the fish take, hold the line tight and the hook will implant itself.

stiffness, both slanted and looped, have all worked with varying degrees of effectiveness. But I was never completely satisfied because there was always a major tradeoff. On the one hand, you face conditions where you need a fly that can slither snag-free through a jungle of vegetation and other potential obstacles. On the other hand, when you draw a strike you want a fly that will ensure a positive hook set. Unfortunately, as if by design, I've found that the more snag resistant the fly, the less effective it is in hooking fish.

Another type of weed guard is this wire configuration popularized by Lefty Kreh. The manner in which the wire is bent in two places aids in hook sets because when a fish bites down, the wire collapses easily.

We had some patterns with weed guards, mostly in the form of monofilament spikes, but even these tended to snag in the vegetation. Bob was determined to try to rectify this. That night back at the lodge he hit on the idea of using a silicone shroud over a top layer of bucktail tied bend-back style. We tied up a few and used them the next day on pike in the weeds and lily pads. Both in terms of being practically snag-free and the ability to plant a hook in the pike's tooth-studded jaw, the fly was an absolute winner. I've yet to find a better weedless pattern and fish this fly everywhere there is snag-infested water, from Florida's backcountry mangroves to Southern California kelp beds.

Thanks to Bob, silicone has become one of my favorite additives for fly tying.

It's relatively inexpensive and readily available, and you can create some amazing effects with it. I use it on everything from feather-duster-size shark and billfish patterns to small inshore bait simulations. An excellent reference for these patterns is Bob and Ed's book *Pop Fleyes* (Stackpole Books, 2001). In addition, I can highly recommend Ed's excellent book for saltwater tiers, appropriately titled *Essential Saltwater Flies* (Stackpole Books, 2007). Ed provides clear color illustrations with accompanying text and tips for tying 38 essential saltwater patterns.

These are the author's saucer-face patterns. The inspiration for them derives from Bob Popovics's Silicone Pop Lip Fly. The saucer shape imparts a darting motion to the fly when it's retrieved using a continuous hand-over-hand stripping technique.

Even when applied sparingly, silicone will enhance a fly's buoyancy, so for those situations where you need to get the fly down quickly, you can facilitate the descent rate by adding weight in the form of weighted eyes (dumbbells), bead chain, split shot, and strands of lead wire that you can buy or strip from lead-core lines like Cortland's Kerplunk, for example.

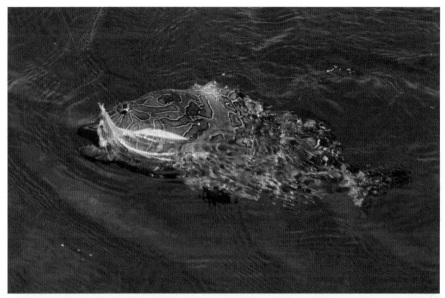

For rock dwellers like this Baja wrasse and golden grouper, weighted flies will generally bring the most action.

For a pattern like the Bendback Silicone, to ensure the fly rides with the hook point facing up, simply take a few turns of lead wire around the shank immediately in front of the bend. Secured in this manner, the remainder of the shank is left bare and the natural appearance of the bucktail wing isn't compromised. Depending on the desired sink rate and hook size, about three to five turns of lead around the shank will handle most conditions.

To maximize hook-setting effectiveness, with a bend-back configuration you want to use a long-shank hook. The Gamakatsu SP11-3LH3 and SS15, Mustad's 34011, and the slightly larger-diameter Wright & McGill 066N (the older version is the 66SS; both are offset, which I straighten with pliers) are hooks I find work well for this. I also use pliers to bend the hook shank. Regardless of the hook brand, for the bend-back style you only want to put a slight downward bend in the shank approximately ¼ inch behind the hook eye.

Any time you apply silicone, it's best to do so using only small dollops at a time. For years I used my finger, but a better way to proceed is to use a narrow wooden coffee stirrer or Popsicle stick. Only apply it in one direction (from the front to the rear), otherwise you'll have a mess. To smooth out the silicone, wipe the applicator clean and take a couple of strokes with a wetting agent like Photo-Flo, soapy water, or saliva.

Of all the talented tiers I know and have spent time with, Bob is the one who has influenced me the most. I stated so quite a number of years back and remain as convinced as ever that he is the most innovative saltwater fly tier on the scene today. Probably the next best thing to sitting next to him at a fly-tying bench is to get a copy of his and Jay Nichols's latest book, *Fleye*

One of the author's Bendback patterns tied with a saucer face fashioned from combed-out macramé cord treated with silicone.

Bob Popovics's Ultra Shrimp is one of the patterns discussed in his new book. He gave me this to fish, but I ended up photographing it instead. Bob now uses Tuffleye in place of epoxy to form the body.

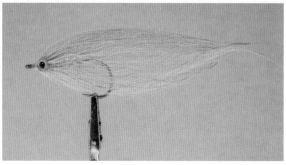

These two flies are baitfish patterns tied with wig hair. They are copies of Bob Popovics's Hollow Fleye that he ties with bucktail.

Design (Stackpole Books, 2016). Whether you're new to the game or have years of experience behind you, you'll find this book to be a great inspiration when you sit at the vise to begin tying.

Just the subject of how Bob works with bucktail to craft his fabulous Bucktail Deceiver and Hollow Fleye is worth the price alone.

For many fly fishers, both fresh and salt, a good deal of the pleasure derived from tying flies lies in the search for new materials either to develop new patterns or improve on old standbys. With the staggering array of consumer goods at our disposal, the quest for useful materials can often begin right at home or the workplace. Bob's initial use of silicone is a good example. In the case of the fly I'm about to describe, the material was staring me in the face for years.

The Macramé Flies

One of the faculty secretaries felt that my office needed a more homey appearance, and she took it upon herself to suspend a couple of hanging plants on either side of one of my bookcases using macramé cord. In a rare moment of creativity that managed to intrude on my daydreaming about a forthcoming trip down to Baja's East Cape, I noticed that the ends of the cords supporting one of the plants were frayed. I don't know why it took so long, but it finally occurred to me that this stuff might be useful for tying streamer patterns. Student research papers were shunted aside that evening as I sat at my tying bench and started to work with a length of cord I liberated from one of the plant containers.

Unraveling the cord was easy, but combing out the fibers proved more time-consuming because I didn't have a suitable tool. A trip to the pet store the following afternoon solved that problem. I bought a wire grooming brush that

A macramé baitfish
pattern

is perfect for this work. In the course of a week I tied about two-dozen flies for the Baja trip and they proved their worth. I caught dorado, jacks, roosterfish, and yellowfin tuna. On one 12-inch-long streamer I hooked a big blue marlin (with fly gear, they are all big), but it shed the fly after the first jump. Over the years striped bass, calico bass, barracuda, bluefish, snook, redfish, roosterfish, yellowtail, yellowfin, and northern pike have all eagerly responded to these macramé patterns, and along with wig hair and Steve Farrar's Flash Blend, I've come to regard it as one of my principal fly-tying materials.

Recently Lily Renzetti introduced me to a material I think will make an excellent addition to these synthetics. It's from South Africa and is marketed as Sculpting Fibre, available in a variety of colors. The material is blended with gold and silver strands and makes for some very enticing baitfish patterns. Aside from not having to comb out the material, tie with it using the same steps for the macramé-type patterns enumerated below.

To complement streamers tied with this material, I am now using the relatively new E-Z Eye system. The eyes come packaged with a series of plastic tabs that are tied in behind the hook eye. They are very easy to set in place; simply stick them to the rounded section of the plastic tab. For demanding saltwater use I recommend coating the eyes with an adhesive like Clear Cure Goo or Tuffleye.

The macramé is a braided polypropylene fiber that is easy to work with, looks great in the water, is durable, and is relatively inexpensive. Increasingly I've found that fewer craft stores are carrying it, so I order what I need online. One brand I like is Bonnie Macrame Braid. A 6 mm (a diameter roughly the size of a wooden pencil) 100-yard skein will generally sell for less than $10. The cord is available in different colors, and there are even multicolored cords. However, I've found that white cord is generally the easiest to unravel and comb out. For different color applications, I use waterproof marking pens.

It's not uncommon when tying a new pattern or working with what you think is a novel material that you are not alone in the enterprise. Such is the case with macramé cord. I first met Ron Winn many years ago at one of the early Shallow Water Expos in Fort Pierce, Florida. A mutual friend, Captain Frank Catino, called me over to where Ron was tying and said, "Nick, you have to check out these flies." I picked up one of his beautifully tied mullet patterns, and Frank and I looked at each and laughed. I don't know who was first and it really doesn't matter, but Ron was no stranger to macramé cord. We compared notes and found that we used a number of the same techniques.

Similar to what Bob Popovics does with many of his bucktail and sheep fleece patterns, I like to apply stick-on eyes to the combed-out macramé.

These can be applied with adhesives such as silicone or brand products like Soft Body, Zap-A-Dap-A-Goo II, Clear Cure Goo, etc.

To achieve a convincing baitfish silhouette, I tie the combed-out material completely around the hook shank in either of two ways Bob has popularized. With his Bucktail Deceiver, Bob ties the bucktail around the shank in the conventional fashion whereby the bucktail butts face toward the hook eye. With his Hollow Fleye pattern, the bucktail is tied in the opposite manner. The natural tapered ends of the bucktail face toward the hook eye.

After the material is completely distributed around the hook shank, a pushing tool (you can use a ballpoint pen cap or ink tube for this) is placed over the hook eye and the bucktail ends are pushed rearward. To achieve the necessary degree of flair, you have to learn to control the amount of tension to apply while wrapping over the material with a fly-tying bobbin. I found this considerably easier to do when using macramé instead of bucktail. Final adjustments to the fly's shape can be made with scissors.

Like other synthetics, macramé cord is not as buoyant as natural bucktail. Nevertheless, especially in a wide-body configuration, it has a rather leisurely sink rate. There are many times this can be deadly, but if you're fishing in strong current and have to get the fly down quickly, wrap the shank with lead wire or use weighted eyes.

The cord I use consists of eight woven strands, and Ron showed me an easy way to unravel it. Select a desired length and begin pulling out the strands one by one. After two or three strands are pulled free, the rest unravel freely and you can begin combing them out. Once all the material is tied on, I like to remove the fly from the vise and grasp the hook eye with a pair of pliers. Now you can easily give the fly a final combing on all sides prior to trimming to the desired shape.

With this material I prefer to use fairly short-shank hooks like the Eagle Claw 254SS (2/0–4/0), the Gamakatsu SC15, the Grip 21711NSL (this is available in a barbless configuration, 21711NSL-BL), the Mustad C68SNP-DT Tarpon, and the Varivas 990. Naturally, the amount of combed-out material you tie on is a function of the size and silhouette you are trying to achieve. For most applications, even on size 2/0 hooks, I generally use six to eight strands of the cord that have been combed out. For smaller baitfish patterns, all you'll need is a single bunch of this material. For large offshore patterns, I seldom stagger more than three bunches. And even if I trim most of it away, it's so inexpensive that I don't feel wasteful.

A rotary vise like a Renzetti greatly facilitates the shaping process. One factor to bear in mind when using synthetics like this is that it will dull your scissors in short order. I use a very inexpensive pair I buy in department stores and repeatedly sharpen the flat, wide blades with a file.

To tie a macramé fly, separate the strands from the main body of cord and comb out the strands with a wire brush. Take a portion of the combed fiber and distribute it around the hook shank just before the bend in the hook. You can use either of Popovics's tying methods described earlier. Depending on the size of the pattern desired, one to three bunches of material are tied on immediately in front of the butt end of the preceding wrap. Trim the fly to the desired profile, color it with the marking pens, and affix the eyes.

The Clouser

The flies you select will vary by locale, of course, but one pattern that has earned nearly universal appeal is the Clouser.

It is easy and quick to tie, a variety of materials can be used, and you can incorporate all sorts of variations in size and color combinations to suit your particular conditions.

As a general guideline for most coastal and inshore fishing, Clousers tied 1 to 3 inches long on size 4 to 2/0 hooks will work well for a wide variety of species. Unless you have a good information source (local fly shops, fly-fishing clubs, and websites like Dan Blanton's Fly Fishing Forum and Bulletin Board/Message Board can be helpful), determining the most productive colors is a matter of putting your time in. If you are not familiar with the area, a good way to begin is to go with all white or white and chartreuse combinations.

Bob Clouser's Clouser Minnow tied by Lefty Kreh, who did much to popularize the pattern.

Rabbit Strip Flies

A pattern similar to the ubiquitous Clouser in terms of its versatility and effectiveness is a simple rabbit strip fly. It sees fairly widespread use in freshwater applications, primarily in the form of a variety of leech patterns, but tends to be overlooked by saltwater fly fishers (a notable exception is the Tarpon Toad, which is a productive fly for many species besides its namesake).

Perhaps one reason it fails to garner more attention is the sheer simplicity of its design. Passing around a box of plain rabbit strip flies to a group who accompanied me on a bonefishing trip to the Bahamas drew comments like "Is that all there is to it?" and "Do these really work?" After a day's fishing, those who offered to give some a try cleaned out my supply of rabbit fur strips so they could tie more for themselves.

Much like marabou, rabbit fur exhibits a scintillating movement in the water that a wide variety of species find very attractive. I've been fishing these patterns since the mid-1980s and they have produced amazingly well on a wide spectrum of game fish in very diverse locales, including the aforementioned Bahamian bonefish flats, California kelp beds, Long Island Sound, and Louisiana bayous. In its most basic form, which is how I normally fish it, the pattern consists of nothing more than a rabbit strip and, if needed, some form of weighting material in the form of lead wire or bead-chain and dumbbell eyes.

One problem with a rabbit strip is its tendency to foul around the hook, but there are ways to help prevent this. A traditional method that has been around for quite some time is to use a monofilament loop or spike to keep the tail from curling around the bend in the hook. However, this requires a hole be punched in the hide to thread the mono through, which I've found can cause the strip to break prematurely.

One alternative I use is to carefully apply an adhesive like Barge Cement, Pliobond, or silicone to the hide from approximately the midpoint of the tail back to where

This simple rabbit strip pattern is effective on a wide variety of species. It is very easy to tie, and the rabbit hairs produce enticing movement in the water.

it extends past the bend in the hook. This stiffens the hide, making it less likely to curl back on itself and foul. Another method is to simply glue the hide along the hook shank back from the hook eye to a point just about at the hook bend. Whichever way you choose, you'll find that the snakelike, pulsating action of a rabbit strip tied in colors and lengths to suit prevailing conditions will draw the attention of practically any game fish you set your sights on. I always try to have a few on hand just about everywhere I fish.

Poppers

No matter where you fish—fresh or saltwater, inshore, offshore—nothing beats the pure adrenaline rush of a surface strike when a thoroughly aroused predator attacks your offering. What makes the experience so compelling is that it can bring into play all four senses. Even if the visual element is compromised, there is usually enough noise to send an emotionally charged signal that high drama is unfolding at the end of your leader.

I have wonderful memories of early summer nights on Long Island's north shore fishing stripers that were smacking sand eels near the surface. The darkest nights when you couldn't even make out the rod tip seemed best, and you definitely had to have your game to fish well in total darkness. But the violent surface strikes when a bass smacked your offering made it all so worthwhile. One of my favorite offerings was Captain Joe Blados's Crease Fly. Back then, as I do now, I fished the original simple design, and it brought me a lot of bass. Technically it's more of a slider than a popper, but with the teardrop-shaped front you can make gentle pops on the surface.

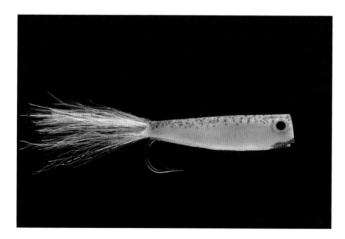

The Blados Crease Fly. Captain Joe originally intended this for topwater applications, but I've also had good success fishing it on a sinking line.

On most of those night trips, you couldn't see what was happening but you certainly heard it. The surface noises could become so pronounced that it became necessary to discipline yourself not to react immediately to the sound of the fish attacking the fly. The trick is to strike only when the line comes tight in your hand and you feel strong resistance. Stripers sometimes will strike a popper with their tail as if they were trying to stun a baitfish, then they'll turn and attempt to make it a meal. Hauling back on the line prematurely based solely on what you see or hear could cause you to miss the fish. Nonetheless, it's a very exciting experience, even when you fail to connect. The surface disturbance may be as subtle as a swirl or as rambunctious as someone executing a cannonball dive. At night all you may have is the sound, but it's more than enough to light up your emotional circuits.

Another memorable instance of sound-driven surface action occurred about a decade ago when a friend and I were hunting yellowfin tuna about 45 miles southwest of Ensenada, Mexico. We spotted seabirds off in the distance but a fog bank was quickly enveloping the area, so he positioned the boat and shut down the engines to allow the current to silently carry us in that direction. It did so and in a matter of minutes the fog was so thick, we could barely make out the bow rail only a few feet away. Soon, however, the blanketed visibility was overshadowed by the sound of tuna intercepting schools of anchovies they had driven to the surface. We cast into the gray, wet shroud and couldn't even see where our poppers landed, but it didn't matter because we were both hooked up immediately to 40-pound-class yellowfin.

The allure of the surface strike is so great that some anglers forgo all subsurface applications. For example, I know a few freshwater buffs that will only fish largemouth bass with poppers. They don't care if sinking presentations produce more fish, it's surface strikes on a popper or nothing

A very effective topwater offering is Todd's Wiggle Minnow, a favorite with South Florida fly fishers.

doing. The closest counterparts to this among saltwater fly fishers I know are those who fish dorado and bluefish almost exclusively on poppers. Of all the saltwater game fish I've pursued, I've found these two species the most prone to pounce on a surface popper.

However, despite the intensity of the fun factor during the take, fishing a popper does have a downside. One major difficulty is learning to cast it properly. Most popper designs tend to be bulky and wind resistant. Add to this the fact that many fly fishers tend to cast too fast with too short a casting stroke. Even a dime-size-diameter popper (and most of those designed for saltwater use are considerably larger than that) is going to have a slowing effect on the travel velocity of the fly line. This means that you will have to adjust the rod movement accordingly.

In any casting situation (even at the other end of the spectrum with fast-sinking shooting heads), a slower controlled stroke is more efficient. But particularly when casting poppers, you want to avoid swinging your arm like you were swatting insects. A lengthened backstroke enables the rod to achieve maximum bend on the forward stroke. When you follow this with a positive, abrupt stop coupled with a short, sharp haul, the result is a nice loop coupled with high line speed that will propel the popper with nearly the same efficiency as you might expect when casting a streamlined baitfish pattern. A common fault that you want to try to avoid here is the tendency to creep forward after you complete the speed-up-and-stop on the backcast. Doing so will bring the rod to an almost vertical position, and there's little space for it to travel except downward on the forward stroke. This directs the fly line downward, and the popper will fall considerably short of the target.

Aside from a poor casting stroke, another fairly common problem begin-ning fly fishers have trying to cast poppers is starting the cast with too short a length of line outside the rod tip (with a floating shooting head, this isn't a problem because the entire head must be outside the rod tip). With too little line outside the tip—say, for example, 15 feet or so—there is not sufficient line weight to carry the popper. When this is the case, the typical response is to make a number of extra false casts to lengthen the line to a point where it can be effectively cast. This is a waste of time and energy.

One strategy to avoid this is to simply stop retrieving the popper at a point where approximately 25 to 30 feet of line is outside the rod tip. Most fish usually don't follow a popper for very long distances (striped bass are one of the exceptions), so it's really not necessary to bring it all the way back in. With a sufficient length of line extending past the rod tip, it's easy to lift the popper from the surface, extend a few more feet of line on the backcast if you need to, and make the forward cast. However, if you retrieve the popper close to you, you'll have to make at least one roll cast or one or two back and forward casts to extend the line so you can make the final forward cast.

A practical leader for use with poppers is one that is fairly short and simple. Oftentimes I use a 3½- to 5-foot level section of 30- to 40-pound-test mono. This works well particularly in windy conditions, and the fact that there are no connecting knots makes it less likely to catch any floating weed or grass. If you are concerned with IGFA leader standards, you'll have to use a section of the desired class tippet size that measures at least 15 inches in length.

When fishing poppers you generally have to resign yourself to the fact that the number of successful hookups is not going to be as high as you might normally expect when using streamer patterns. Often you just have to chalk it up to the fact that the fish simply missed its target. Predators, whether they are grizzlies swiping salmon from the rapids or tuna targeting terrified pods of baitfish, have to be efficient, otherwise they simply do not survive. But that doesn't mean they always connect with their prey. Some are more successful than others but they all experience misses, and that's the case with the game fish we set our sights on. Spend enough time presenting poppers to your targeted species, and you'll begin to accumulate memories of dramatic surface displays where fish crashed your artificial and you came up empty-handed.

Mother Nature's shortcomings aside, failure to effect a successful hook-up with poppers often lies on the angler's side of the equation and can be blamed on two factors: improper technique and faulty popper design. As far as technique is concerned, a very common mistake anglers make when trying to hook a fish on a popper is using the rod to manipulate the offering by flipping the tip upward. Following the law that what goes up must come down, when the tip is lowered slack is created in the line, and the simple fact is that you cannot effectively make a hook penetrate with loose line.

A related problem is using the rod to strike the fish. A more effective tactic is to keep the tip low to the water and strike by sharply pulling back on the line. And as stated above, try to avoid relying on the visual and audio elements alone. Only strike when you actually feel resistance against the line in your stripping hand, then make a short, sharp pull backwards. This way if the fish misses the popper, with the rod tip still close to the surface with a tight line, you're in an ideal position to set up on the fish if it decides to take another shot at it.

The Evolution of a New Popper Design

Despite your skill level, proper technique will not yield an optimum number of successful hookups if the popper you are fishing suffers from design flaws. Typically the defect lies in a reduced hook gap width. The gap, also referred to as the throat, is the distance between the hook point and the bottom of the shank directly above the point. A narrow gap compromises your ability to set the hook on the strike. Even if you manage to stick the fish, the connection is often short-lived because a small gap does not penetrate deeply and the fish is soon able to rid itself of this temporary annoyance. Too often on commercially tied poppers the hook shank is buried too deep in the popper's body, creating too narrow a gap.

The material a popper is constructed from also has an effect on its performance. One obvious consideration is to select ones that are constructed of the lightest material possible. Cork- and balsa-bodied poppers are traditional choices, but closed-cell foam is even lighter. Also with cork and balsa poppers, fish often try to eject it because they do not compress like most natural prey. The ones that are embossed with layers of paint and lacquer may look great, but the billiard ball finish is not only unnecessary, it can also render the popper heavier than it need be.

A related flaw is a popper that has too much material affixed to the hook shank immediately behind the body. Again, this is a flaw to be alert for with some commercially tied poppers that have palmered hackle between the tail and rear portion of the body. All this does is increase air resistance. In addition, long trailing tail hackles can foul as well as add unnecessary weight. A sparse bunch of bucktail is the ideal choice for the popper's tail.

The difficulties mentioned above, along with the fact that I am so drawn to fishing a popper even under circumstances where it may not be the most practical choice, served as motivation to try to develop a more effective bug. The Crease Fly was the inspiration for my Catamaran popper that evolved into what I refer to as the Low Rider system.

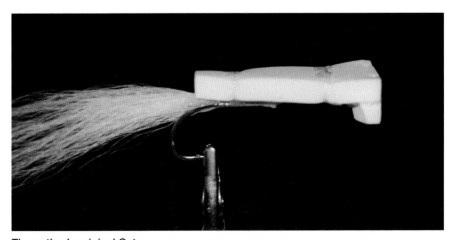

The author's original Catamaran popper.

Like Captain Joe Blados, I chose foam for the body material instead of balsa or cork, because it is lighter and lends itself more easily to different design concepts. Also because it is soft, I'm convinced that fish tend not to reject it as readily when they clamp down on it. I experimented with many different shapes before hitting on the idea of a catamaran profile. I recalled watching a catamaran sailboat plow through nasty chop and hit on the idea of incorporating this profile for a different popper design.

The body is cut from $1/4$-inch-thick foam readily available at most craft stores. The form is roughly a triangular shape with a $1\frac{1}{4}$-inch length. The front face is $3/4$ inch wide, tapering to $1/2$ inch at the rear. Two square $3/16$-inch foam nubs are glued at each end to the underside of the body. These dimensions are suitable for a wide range of freshwater (e.g., largemouth and smallmouth bass, pike) as well as inshore saltwater species (calico bass, striped bass, medium-size yellowtail, dorado, roosterfish, school tuna, etc.) and can be easily altered to suit specific needs.

Relative to its size, this popper casts remarkably well. It is lightweight, and unlike traditional full-body designs, it offers little in the way of air resistance. Additionally, and perhaps even more important, is the fact that the hook is positioned flush with the underbelly of the popper and the face of the popper. This affords two advantages: First, because the hook shank is not buried deep in the popper body, you have maximum hook-setting effectiveness. Second, the popper is very easy to lift from the surface. It doesn't dig into the water when you're picking it up in preparation for the backcast, a common problem with many traditional popper designs.

Despite all the advances in synthetics, I still find that plain bucktail makes for the best tail material on poppers. Unencumbered and devoid of feathers, bucktail yields a sleek, aerodynamic profile, which makes it relatively easy to cast.

Finally, the unique Catamaran face affords a maximum of fish-stimulating surface commotion requiring a bare minimum of line manipulation. If you want a full-blown disturbance, all you do is make a short, sharp tug on the line. This will cause the popper to simultaneously spray water, belch, and create a surface splash. In contrast, if a more subdued presentation is desired, a steady hand-over-hand retrieve will result in an enticing subtle surface wake that I've found very effective on twilight stripers, backwater snook, and redfish.

Captain Jim White was the first to witness this popper in action. It was around mid-August and the concentration of blues and stripers began to expand along coastal Rhode Island, almost as if they were intentionally gathering for the anticipated annual fall blitz. Jim's first comment when I handed him the popper was, "I've never seen anything like this—does it work?" I told him we would soon find out.

We caught the peak of an outgoing tide not far off Goddard State Park, which makes for ideal conditions for testing the action of a surface offering. A baitfish-shaped pattern like the Crease Fly will work particularly well when you retrieve it downcurrent because it snakes across the surface with a minimum of water disturbance. In contrast, most traditional poppers seem to perform best when they are manipulated against the current flow, where they can effect the most surface commotion. But as Jim soon discovered, the beauty of the Catamaran design is that it can create a very effective measure of surface disturbance anywhere you work it—downcurrent, upcurrent, or crosscurrent, all with a minimum of line manipulation. After a half-dozen or so casts, he said, "This thing splashes like my grandson in the wading pool, and spits more water than a baseball dugout."

It was one of those banner days in the Northeast where we were on to fish for about three consecutive hours. Schools of voracious, blitzing bluefish made up the bulk of our catch that day, and to be perfectly honest, when these feeding machines go into a frenzy, they'll eat practically anything you put in front of them. In that sense, I wasn't convinced that these fish provided any clear evidence as to the Catamaran's attractive qualities. However, a more accurate confirmation was established when we slid into a quiet cove and coaxed two nice bass that were laid up close to the shoreline. With the first striper it only took one gentle tug on the line to bring the popper to life. It belched like a rude "frat cat," shot out a stream of water, and disappeared in a violent froth. The second bass intercepted the popper when it was about a third of the way back to the boat. Jim shouted about the wake coming up behind the popper, and seconds later the bulge of water changed into that telltale swirl and we could see the striper's silver flanks as it turned with the popper in the corner of its jaw.

For the next outing a few weeks afterward, I had my sights on false albacore. Characteristic of the tuna clan, they can engage in some very dramatic feeding frenzies but at the same time also prove to be maddeningly selective. A number of my very skilled fly-tying friends have spent countless hours at the bench trying to devise various baitfish patterns that appeal to these "Fat Alberts" when they're feeding on the real thing. My good friend Iain Sorrell is well acquainted with these albie antics, and after an hour or so of unsuccessfully trying to coax them with our diminutive baitfish patterns, he suggested I try presenting one of the Catamaran poppers I had in my fly box. Surprisingly, it accounted for the only two albies we boated that trip.

We arrived late at one spot the albies just vacated and decided to shut the engine and wait to see if they would pop up close to where we were drifting. There were no birds dive-bombing the surface, and I wasn't very confident there were any albacore in the area. Consequently, I didn't focus too intently on what I was doing, basically just going through the motions of casting and retrieving the popper. I never saw the fish hit. All I felt was the line suddenly come tight in my hand. I struck back with my line hand, and the stripping basket was quickly emptied of its contents. At first I thought I connected with a big bluefish, but as line continued disappearing from the spool, my thoughts turned to false albacore. Iain was of the same mind when he shouted, "It's got to be an albie, mate!" Eventually, when it began that characteristic circle dance in the depths, we saw that it was in fact an albie.

After landing and releasing the fish, we began searching the area again. I was thinking about changing back to a small baitfish pattern, but Iain encouraged me to stick with the popper for a while. Eventually we managed to slide into breaking fish, and once again, one decided to eat the popper. There were two other boats casting to the breaks but no bent rods as the school suddenly vanished, leaving birds as well as anglers hungry for more action.

Moving up the tuna ladder, on two separate occasions chasing bluefin off Rhode Island, I had three fish take the popper when all the streamers patterns failed to draw strikes. Unfortunately, I failed to land any. One was cut off by an overeager angler who came in too close to where we were fishing, and the other two wore through the 30-pound-test bite tippet.

Tying the Catamaran Popper

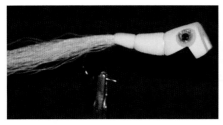 

Rainy's Catamaran Popper

Materials

Hook:	#1/0-3/0 long-style hook similar to the ones I use for bend-back patterns discussed earlier in the chapter (Gamakatsu SP11-3L3H3, Gamakatsu SS15, Wright & McGill 066N, and Mustad 34011)
Thread:	White flat waxed nylon
Tail:	Bucktail
Body:	¼-inch-thick closed-cell foam

The original Catamaran popper is simply a fixed-hook version of the Low Rider. The tail material (bucktail or synthetic) is tied on top of the hook shank near the rear portion of the hook.

For the body cut a 1¼-inch length of ¼-inch-thick foam to a modified triangle shape. The front face should be approximately ¾ inch wide. The width of the rear section is approximately ½ inch. As depicted in the photos below, cut two small nubs of foam approximately ³⁄₁₆ inch square and glue to each side of the front underside of the foam body.

I like to use superglue to affix the foam body to the top of the hook shank. Make sure the front face of the body extends past the hook eye by about ¼ inch. For extra security you can take three or four turns of thread around the rear portion of the

This is a front and bottom view of the Catamaran popper body. It is the same as the Low Rider body save for the fact that it doesn't incorporate the plastic tube as shown.

foam body. Do not wind the thread too tightly, as it might cut into the foam. You can make another few turns with the thread around the body behind the hook eye.

The Low Rider

I fished this popper in its original Catamaran design for about eight years with very good results, but became interested in a tube fly design when Captain Scott Leon showed me some of his patterns he was fishing in the San Diego kelp beds. I seldom tied or fished any tube flies, but he was having very good results so I decided to modify the popper.

Instead of affixing the hook shank directly to the underside of the foam, I glued a length of ³⁄₁₆-inch-diameter clear plastic tubing to run the leader through. A variety of tubing material will work, but I prefer the plastic type. The size of the inside diameter may also vary, but I want it small enough to prevent the hook's eye from sliding inside it. If this happens the hook may lodge in such a way that the point is oriented sideways or doesn't ride point up. With the hook eye riding behind the tube, the hook remains entirely free of the popper body, so there is nothing in the way to interfere with its penetration capabilities and the Low Rider configuration casts as easily as the Catamaran predecessor. Also because the body slides away from the trailing hook, it seldom gets damaged even when fishing tooth-studded species like bluefish.

The fact that the hook point rides up bend-back style on the streamer portion of the popper helps mitigate potential snags, making the popper a good choice for waters laden with obstructions like grass and weeds. I tied some for Lefty Kreh, who fished them on a smallmouth trip in grass-choked water and found that with a vigorous backcast the flat body easily shed the debris. Equally important, with the addition of a few wraps of lead around the shank, the hook point will sit low in the water below the popper body, which greatly increases the ability to make a positive hook set.

As with any popper, you have to consider how much surface commotion is appropriate for the conditions and species you are fishing. Usually in areas where there is already considerable water movement (fishing in rip currents or the boiling surf are good examples), maximum action may be the hot ticket and this popper setup will deliver. A sharp tug on the line will create all the "pop" and noise you'll need. On the other end of the continuum, a slow-paced hand-over-hand retrieve will swim the popper across the surface, creating an enticing wake with minimum noise or disturbance. I found this to be very successful for fish like stripers and snook that are lying in relatively shallow water.

Tying the Low Rider

1. Cut the foam body and nubs using the same dimensions as the Catamaran popper.

To create the bend-back hook shape, grasp the hook approximately ¼ inch behind the hook eye with a pair of pliers and gently push down on the shank. What you're trying to do is create a slight bend downward, not a sharp angle. Take a few wraps around the shank below the hook point with some small-diameter lead.

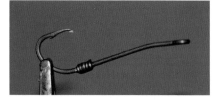

A long-shank hook bent bend-back style with lead wraps to make it sink behind the popper body.

I use superglue to secure it in place. You can also wrap over this with tying thread.

2. Tie the pattern you like. Just be sure to keep it relatively sparse and take care that the material is tied on the underside of the hook shank (the hook is inserted into the tying vise with the hook point facing up). This will ensure that the hook point will always ride up.

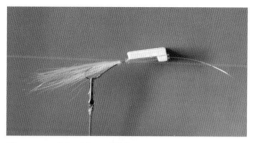

The completed Low Rider popper.

It does work. This is a striper that fell for it in the California Delta.

As I stated at the beginning of this chapter, because I derive so much pleasure catching fish on flies I tied myself, I seldom use flies tied by others. When someone far more talented than myself gives me one of their creations, I always worry about losing it. In the event I lose one of my own to a fish, I still have the satisfaction that it was at least good enough to elicit a strike. Success can come in increments, and partial success is better than complete failure.

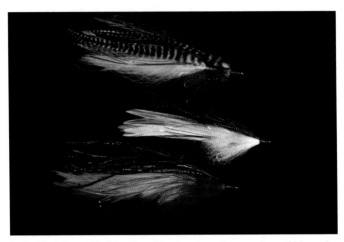

Lefty Deceivers tied by Dan Blanton in various colors. Although it remains one of the best baitfish imitations you can put in front of a fish, the fact remains that it is only an imitation. But when a fish is deceived into mistaking it for the real thing, your satisfaction level rises considerably.

INDEX